PHILOSOPHY

An Outline for the Intending Student

CONTRIBUTORS

R. J. Hirst

D. R. Bell

W. H. Walsh

R. W. Hepburn

H. B. Acton

PHILOSOPHY

An Outline for the Intending Student

Edited by

R. J. Hirst
Professor of Logic
University of Glasgow

ROUTLEDGE & KEGAN PAUL
LONDON, HENLEY AND BOSTON

First published 1968
by Routledge & Kegan Paul Ltd
39 Store Street
London WC1E 7DD,
Broadway House, Newtown Road
Henley-on-Thames
Oxon RG9 1EN and
9 Park Street
Boston, Mass. 02108, USA
Reprinted 1970, 1973 and 1978
Printed in Great Britain by
Lowe & Brydone Printers Limited, Thetford, Norfolk

ISBN 0 7100 6099 8

CONTENTS

PREFACE

While one needs to read all the five chapters in this book to get a balanced introduction to philosophy, there will no doubt be some who will wish to look first at what is said on certain parts of philosophy or certain philosophical questions which interest them most. This is quite feasible (though it is advisable to read the Introduction first), and to facilitate it I have allowed a little repetition of important points and have given cross-references to passages in other contributions where some term or point is more fully discussed. A few questions are raised by more than one writer, and the acute reader may detect a slight difference in emphasis between the two treatments. One can hardly expect or exact complete uniformity from a group of philosophers (or indeed of economists, historians, literary critics or scientists), and the different emphases are beneficial in revealing different aspects of the topic and different possibilities of evaluation; they certainly should not be enough to cause any confusion in the reader.

I am above all indebted to the contributors for their prompt and willing co-operation, but I should also like to thank those of my colleagues who have given advice, and especially Professor W. G. Maclagan for his helpful comments on the editorial chapters.

R. J. HIRST

I

Introduction

R. J. Hirst

Aim of the book

While intended to help anyone who is wondering what philosophy is, this book is particularly meant for those sixth-formers and first-year undergraduates who are considering the possibility of taking philosophy as part of a university course. Our aim is to explain the nature of philosophy by giving the reader some grasp of a few key philosophical problems and of the way in which they are formulated and tackled. By thus entering into some typical philosophical issues as deeply as is possible in a brief book, we hope to enable the intending student to understand more readily what is involved in studying philosophy and so form a sounder decision than would otherwise be possible about whether the subject is for him.

There seems to be a clear need for a book of this sort. Philosophy is not a school subject, and while this may save it from some of the prejudices with which those studying languages at school view the sciences and vice versa, it does mean that the sixth-former may not have ready access to advice from anyone who has studied the subject. And yet at the same time a number of universities which have three-year honours courses (mainly the older English provincial ones) require undergraduates to decide on their main honours subject before entry to the university. Prospective philosophy students are thus faced with a decision vital to their subsequent careers when they normally lack the proper knowledge on which to base this decision. Consequently many who would have enjoyed and profited from a philosophical course play safe by choosing subjects with which they have some acquaintance, while others may be deterred from philosophy by such misconceptions as that one needs to be good at mathematics, or may pick on a philosophical course as the result of quite mistaken notions about its nature. And even in those universities such as the Scottish ones where the final decision on a philosophical course need not be taken until the end of the first or second year of study at the university, by which time the student may indeed have been able to take a year of the subject to find out how it suits him, there is nevertheless evidence that these misunderstandings occur.

It is worth while dwelling for a moment on some of the wrong reasons that may tempt a student to opt for the study of philosophy. Some choose it because they have lost their religious faith and think it will provide a substitute, while some may look to it for a defence of that faith; others think it will solve personal moral problems as though the moral philosopher were a Father Confessor or Aunt Marjorie; others again have been attracted by what they have heard of some grandiose metaphysical scheme which claims to reveal the ultimate Reality or lay bare the secret springs of human character and action. Any who approach the subject for these reasons may be disappointed; for while philosophy does examine and assess attempts at a rational justification of moral principles and of belief in God, the careful analytical methods which characterise it today are too abstract and detached to provide personal spiritual comfort, too prosaic and unadventurous to satisfy the need for uplifting speculation. True there are important elements in the great systems of the past which have a perennial appeal and are an inspiration to thinkers in every generation, but experience has shown that there are fatal flaws in all ambitious speculative schemes, so that a more cautious step-by-step approach is required. So while there are both excitement and satisfaction in the study of philosophy, they are of a rather different kind. There is aesthetic pleasure in the appreciation of a beautifully constructed system of ideas or an ingenious proof, and indeed an earthier pleasure in defeating some opponent in discussion, but the main appeal is more intellectual—the satisfaction in finding the solution to a problem, in the refutation of an argument, in the justification of a thesis, or in the dispelling of a confusion.

We have mentioned these misconceptions because to read a book like this one before being committed is as important for those who think they understand what philosophy is, as it is for those who don't know, and know that they don't know.

Method adopted

There are many introductions to philosophy, but they are normally written as textbooks or as source books, i.e. as aids to study for those embarked on the subject, and therefore must cover a lot of ground fairly thinly—much more ground than is needed to illustrate philosophical problems and methods. To make it easier for the beginner to discover what goes on in philosophy a more selective approach is needed. We have therefore adopted a sampling method, with contributors concentrating on one or two typical problems in their branch of philosophy and treating these in as great a depth as space allows. An exception is in the discussion of Logic, since its particular problems are technical and presuppose an understanding of its basic ideas. A simple general exposition of some of these has therefore been attempted in the first half of Chapter 2. By contrast, Chapter 4 is doubly a sample in that it gives an example of philosophical debate, as well as discussing two typical problems in moral philosophy. We shall try to show why these problems are problems, why they are worth studying, and what the main lines of tackling them are. Nevertheless some initial guide lines are necessary, some indication of the common features of these different problems which make them all philosophical, and this is something that this introduction will attempt to supply.

In accordance with the general plan of this series of introductory books, each chapter is the work of a different philosopher, an expert in his particular field. This is not meant to imply that the book enters regions of knowledge so remote that a team of specialists is required; rather the point is that each contributor is practised in explaining his particular field to beginners. Writing introductory books is in many ways more difficult than writing for professionals, so in this sense an expert is required—one who by long experience has acquired the art of putting over some aspect of philosophy.

There is the further advantage that this procedure enables us to draw on a wide range of experience of different universities. This is important because there are many different courses and options available in philosophy in British universities. Furthermore there are certain differences in emphasis (for instance the history of philosophy is generally more prominent in Scotland than in many English universities). At one time even there were marked differences in conception of philosophy. The development of analytical methods, the so-called 'revolution in philosophy', at first led those philosophers who adopted them to despise others as old-fashioned metaphysicians, while they were in turn accused of just playing with words. Happily, this acrimony has largely disappeared, and a roughly similar conception of philosophy is to be found in all British universities. But this may not be realised by those who were introduced to philosophy in the period of this revolution just after the Second World War and then lost professional contact with it. Consequently, for they may be advisers of intending students, we have taken great care not to seem parochial. Thus, while to ease the editor's task all contributors are university teachers in Edinburgh and Glasgow, they have in fact a wide background of experience. All graduated at different universities from those they now teach in, and they include a former Oxford don (W. H. Walsh), former professors at London (H. B. Acton) and Nottingham (R. W. Hepburn), and former lecturers at Manchester (D. R. Bell) and St. Andrews (R. J. Hirst). Further, we have colleagues who hail from other universities on whose experience we have been able to draw.

Finally the book includes a chapter on practical points which we hope will be of assistance to the intending student.

This comprises: (i) a brief classified list of introductory books on philosophy; (ii) a discussion of the general and formal requirements for the study of philosophy; (iii) brief comments on modes of instruction and study; (iv) a discussion of the university courses available in philosophy, with some advice on the considerations to be borne in mind in choosing a university, and on how to get the necessary detailed information; (v) a note on careers. Parents at least are apt to worry about what on earth anyone can do when they have got a philosophy degree. While openings are limited compared to those provided by some other subjects, so is the number of philosophy graduates; and it is hoped that this note will be of some assistance to those who would like to study the subject.

What is philosophy?

Several difficulties face any attempt to provide students with a definition or succinct account of philosophy. One is that the word has been current for so long that many erroneous notions may already have prejudiced them. Some errors we have mentioned in discussing the wrong reasons for choosing to study it. Philosophy is no longer (at least in British universities) the construction of imposing theories about the nature of the universe or the attempt to reveal the true reality behind a veil of misleading appearances; nor does it aim at providing the solution to personal problems. Equally misleading is the popular usage, 'He took it philosophically'—do not expect the philosophy professor to accept a late or shoddy essay with calm resignation. Nor is etymology much help: 'philosophy' is Greek for 'love of wisdom', but few philosophers would claim to love wisdom any more than the next man.

A more serious difficulty is that the philosophers themselves are not fully agreed on a definition; for any such definition is likely to have implications about what they should study or how they should tackle the subject, and all these have been a matter of dispute between rival schools of thought. But there is enough common ground for one to be able to help the enquirer by stating briefly what philosophy is, at least as taught in British universities today, even though any definition needs to be accompanied by a good deal of explanation.

One fairly common view would be that philosophy is the rational investigation of certain fundamental problems about the nature of man and the world he lives in. This is only a starting-point, however, since it turns on two unclear terms 'certain' and 'fundamental'. The first of these merely indicates that philosophy does not concern itself with every problem that might be called fundamental, and 'fundamental' itself is vague, often being used only to indicate that the speaker thinks the problems important. So to clarify this we need to give examples of philosophical problems and indicate what makes them philosophical, how they differ from for example scientific or theological ones. In a sense, the whole book is an attempt to do this, for the contributors are considering typical problems; but we can give a preliminary selection here. The first two groups of problems will be developed in Chapter 3, the next two in Chapter 4, while the last introduces the themes of Chapter 2.

What is the true nature of a person or human being? What is it that distinguishes him from other animals and from computers? It is not just his looks or appearance, for one need not read science fiction to be able to imagine a robot with human form. Is it then that human beings have minds or souls—but what are minds or souls? One traditional answer is that a mind or soul is a spiritual being, lodged in and directing a physical body in this life, but essentially different from it and capable of existing apart from it after death. Since the body is thus regarded as secondary and inessential, this view amounts to saying that the true person, the real 'you' or 'I', is a spiritual non-material being of this kind. Others say that the soul is a religious myth without rational foundation, and that talk about a person's mind is just a way of indicating certain abilities, states and activities: 'He has an acute mind' means he is very clever; 'He is in two minds' or 'can't make up his mind' means he is undecided and so on. Thus what distinguishes human beings is the complexity of their abilities and behaviour; they are just physical organisms of a particularly elaborate kind and have evolved from simpler ones. Others again might temper that view by saying that human beings are characterised by mind in the sense of consciousness—thus it is their awareness, particularly of themselves as individuals, their experiences, emotions and thoughts which distinguish them, even though all these are special abilities of the human brain and die with it. How then can we decide between even these few proposals?—and of course there are many more.

Is there a God? What is he like? Is there a divine purpose in the world? Is the world created and founded by some supreme being or is it just a fortuitous concourse of atoms, something that just is, or has happened, by chance? Many religions offer answers, but their answers rely on revelation or the authority of some teacher. The philosophical interest is rather in the search for a rationally based answer, i.e. can we *prove* that God exists, or that there is no God? Also nowadays there is quite a lot of philosophical discussion of what we *mean* when talking about God.

Another well-known and difficult problem is that of free will; so notorious, indeed, that Milton in *Paradise Lost* (II, 550) portrayed some of the fallen angels as philosophising on this problem and finding 'no end, in wandering mazes lost'. We all believe that we are free to choose between alternative courses of action. Of course the choice may be limited by disease or imprisonment or lack of money, but for most people it is quite wide. Even if we obey the law or other authority we feel we could have defied it if necessary, and if we break a rule or do wrong we would normally admit that the responsibility was ours because we could have done otherwise. Now this conviction of freedom seems to clash with various apparent facts. Thus some have thought that science shows everything is subject to strict physical laws: the position and movement of all the atoms in the universe, including those that make up our brain and bodies, are determined by physical law so that free choice of action is illusory. Again, others have claimed that fate or destiny governs our actions, or that God has foreknowledge of them

—and if God knows what we will do how can we choose to do otherwise? Or again, our make up is the product of heredity and environment, and so our decision isn't really free because it is governed by our genes and by the influences which moulded us in childhood.

Let us turn to problems of conduct. Why should one do one's duty, why should one obey the law, if one can get away with it? Or if that sounds rather cynical, one might ask just how one should try to defend a belief that the H-bomb is wicked, or how to convince a white South African that *apartheid* is wrong. To what can one appeal? Are there any universally accepted principles of right and wrong, or is it a matter of individual tastes and attitudes?

We have said that philosophy is a *rational* investigation of these problems, i.e. it accepts conclusions only after careful examination of reasons and evidence. And we have already seen how these problems involve questions of justifying principles or proving things. So one very important set of philosophical problems concern standards and methods of proofs, ways of testing arguments, criteria of evidence and of satisfactory explanations and justifications—questions of logic in fact. Furthermore, even to understand the questions asked, let alone test solutions, one has to grasp the meanings of the words used and clarify the ideas involved; this kind of analysis is a vital part of philosophy. Along with these questions are raised others—epistemological ones—about the nature and criteria of the knowledge one hopes to achieve (How does one know that one knows? What is truth?) and about the ways of getting evidence and knowledge: for example, observation by the senses is a common one, but is it wholly trustworthy? May not eyes and ears deceive us?

From these examples we can see some characteristics of philosophical problems. First, their generality or wide scope. Philosophy is not a detailed study like microbiology or plasma physics; it discusses broad questions whose consideration involves many different things and cuts across boundary lines that divide other subjects. (For more on this, with reference to metaphysics, see p. 57). Thus to discuss mind/body questions one might have to bring in some facts from neurology (what happens in the brain?), electronics (computers and their achievements), psychology (experimental study of human behaviour), the arts (since, despite some rash claims on behalf of chimpanzees and computers, artistic creation seems something distinctively human), or theology (for certain doctrines about the soul). Quite a formidable list! Only a few points however will be involved from each and most of the time will be directed to clarifying concepts like 'mind' and 'person', and to examining the various theories that have been put forward. One consequence of this fact that philosophical problems are more general than others and that all sorts of evidence may be relevant, is that the more one knows about other subjects the better one is likely to progress in philosophy: one is more likely to get a proper and well-balanced view and less tempted to talk nonsense—even clever nonsense.

Secondly, philosophy is general in another way, in that it is concerned with principles and problems at a relatively high level of abstraction. It is asking not the real nature of Tom or Dick, so much as that of man in general, not about Jack's mind or Jim's but about any human mind, not about whether one should visit a sick friend or pay £x by the 15th, but about duties and promises as such. Examples of course are discussed, but only as illustrations of general principles. With this goes impartiality and objectivity, i.e. philosophy is no respecter of persons and condemns special pleading or any pretence that the principles you would expect others to accept do not apply in your particular case.

Thirdly, it should be clear from the examples that the main philosophical problems are indeed fundamental; they concern the principles on which depend our conception of man and his place in the world, and so also our values, i.e. what we judge to be good and important. Any fully rational plan of life, in which we know what we are doing and why, must be governed ultimately by our beliefs about the nature of man and of morality, or about whether there is a God or our actions are free, i.e. must depend on answers to the central philosophical questions. Furthermore, advanced study of the sciences soon reaches a point in which one asks questions about the basic concepts or presuppositions involved, e.g. about 'law' or 'cause' or 'reality' or 'identity', questions which are philosophical, though professional philosophers have no monopoly in discussing them.

On the other hand one must not exaggerate the role of philosophical enquiry in practical matters. Our life is not lived in isolation; our society, and in particular our home, church and school background are based on a set of answers to these questions which provide a foundation for everyday life that is normally quite adequate in practice. Thus many people lead happy and blameless lives without ever having seriously raised philosophical questions—they are quite content with the conventional answers of their society or religion. Still, if one is to be fully adult, i.e. is to use one's reason and intelligence to the full, one must make an independent decision after considering the evidence and basic principles involved. This requires effort, but then even the sheep-like following of convention is no guarantee of contentment; the rub comes when one is faced with a clash between traditional answers or between one's conventional background and one's own feelings. This may be forced on anyone any time by some crisis, which may be national (e.g. is it right for the country to make a stand at the risk of atomic war?) or personal—if one's grandfather contracts a painful incurable cancer, is euthanasia allowable? if one falls in love, is sex before marriage all right? Philosophy, of course, does not claim to give answers to these questions in a way a politician or a priest does, but if one is to give a rational answer to them, one cannot get very far without raising those general and fundamental questions which are philosophical. And though philosophy does not provide final or even agreed answers to these basic questions themselves, it does clarify the issues and show what are the main views that have been put forward, and what are their strong and weak points, i.e. it puts one in a position to make a personal evaluation and decision. Indeed a good deal of philosophical discussion is concerned with the preliminaries, i.e. with analysing the questions, with deciding the best method of approach and the criteria of acceptable answers.

A fourth characteristic of philosophical problems is that they cannot be solved by empirical or scientific methods, i.e. by observation and experiment. This in fact, along with the wide scope mentioned earlier, is what distinguishes them from scientific ones. (Indeed what we call science was once part of philosophy, but as various topics became subject to experimental methods of enquiry or improved modes of observation, they split off from philosophy and developed independently.) The psychologist, for example, can observe a person's behaviour or devise experiments to discover on what factors judgement of distance depends; but the philosopher cannot learn from observation whether the mind is a spiritual entity, or design experiments to decide whether we have free will; observables such as behaviour stay the same whichever theory is correct. Similarly a social scientist may do a Gallup Poll and discover that say 60 per cent of the population think that hanging should be abolished, but counting heads does not show that hanging is right or wrong. Thus although there is some overlap in problems between philosophy and science, they differ in that philosophy has little chance of empirical investigation and relies wholly on analytical and logical examination. There is some overlap with theological problems also, but philosophy differs here in that it is not committed. It is not making enquiries to justify a certain world view or to develop its consequences, but it advances without fear or favour to find whatever theory is best supported and justified.

With these explanations then, we can say that philosophy is the rational investigation of fundamental, highly general, problems about man, the world, and his conduct in it. Often this definition is put a little differently, however. One well-known work says that philosophy is 'critical reflection on the justification of basic human beliefs and analysis of basic concepts in terms of which such beliefs are expressed'. (P. Edwards and A. Pap, *A Modern Introduction to Philosophy*.) But this is really just a difference of emphasis: it is one that has the advantage of pointing to philosophical practice—philosophers are continually examining beliefs and criticising ideas. On the other hand the beliefs concern the fundamental questions we have distinguished, and the analysis of concepts (which we discuss further p. 13), if it is not to be just idle or for sharpening the wits, must be directed at the clarification of these problems. We have therefore preferred to place our emphasis on the problems, the ultimate subject-matter of philosophical enquiry.

Philosophical methods

How then does philosophy proceed if not by observation and experiment? Some illustration of the actual use of its methods is given in the main chapters of this book. Essentially philosophy is a rational or critical investigation of problems, and this means that it involves continual testing and probing. This starts with the questions themselves, for it is all too easy to waste time by trying to answer unanswerable questions or failing to see assumptions that are implied in the question. For example, one might ask: 'What is the correct treatment for a juvenile delinquent?' or 'What is the right way to bring up children?' But there is obviously not the one answer which the word 'the' suggests, because individual circumstances vary. The most notorious example of implied assumptions is non-philosophical, that of the lawyer who asked, 'Have you stopped beating your wife? Don't prevaricate, answer me "yes" or "no" '. The philosophical cases are usually much less clear cut and are open to controversy, but one can claim as examples of loaded questions. 'How are past experiences stored in the mind?' (Are they stored?). 'How does the mind interact with the body?' (Does it? is there a *mind* which can interact?). 'Why should I do my duty?' (Some say this is sensible, others say that as 'It is your duty' is the final answer to 'Why should I?' questions, to ask this of duty itself is like saying, 'Is the standard metre really a metre long? Let's measure it and see'). But apart from analysing the question itself, all the common beliefs and philosophical theories which can be regarded as answers to it must be examined. Nothing is to be accepted on trust or without a justification (even if sometimes the justification has to be that one is dealing with something ultimate and self evident, though that is only accepted after much discussion). These examinations involve the following procedures.

Conceptual analysis. A concept is a general idea (one applicable to a class of things of the same kind) e.g. man or triangle; in particular an abstract general idea (i.e. not of something concrete or picturable) e.g. democracy or progress. But analysing concepts is not quite the same as clarifying one's ideas, for what is analysed is not something personal and private but is objective and shared by many people. This makes it a difficult and controversial question what a concept really is (is it mental even?), but fortunately for practical purposes we can treat 'concept of X' as equivalent to 'meaning of the word "X" ', so that analysing concepts amounts to examination and clarification of the meanings of the terms used, e.g. if it is a question about mind, then one asks what is meant by 'mind'? What do we understand by it? What features do we require before we say someone has a mind or a certain type of mind etc? Are there hidden ambiguities, assumptions or confusing vagueness in the use of the word and so on?

Logical analysis. Is the reasoning used in arguments and proofs sound? Are there dubious implicit premisses?

Testing of hypotheses and suggested solutions. Are they clear, precise? Are they consistent with other beliefs? Are they comprehensive, covering all the facts? Are they economical, i.e. do they make the least number of assumptions? (If you explain a fault in a plane by saying that it is due to gremlins, that is uneconomical because it postulates the existence of mysterious beings when the fault can be explained on the basis of accepted scientific principles.)

Checking evidence and matters of fact appealed to. Are they genuine facts, i.e. not mistaken? do they really support the case or are there alternative explanations?

One must not suppose that philosophy is wholly a critical

examination of questions and beliefs; that would make it seem purely negative and destructive. Philosophy is after all seeking solutions to fundamental problems and so the criticism is meant to lead to better answers; and the greatest philosophers have all put forward positive theories in an attempt to deal with these problems, even though sometimes the positive contribution consists in saying that the problem is not genuine or must be completely restated and then dealt with by science.

An undergraduate course must involve study and practice of these techniques of philosophy, particularly the methods of analysing meanings or of testing arguments; it must introduce a wide range of philosophical problems and show the merits and demerits of the main attempts at their solution. A philosophy student will also have set books, i.e. be expected to read and study works of past philosophers like Plato, Descartes, Locke, Berkeley and Hume, or, at an advanced level, Kant. This is not antiquarian zeal on the part of those who designed the syllabus. There are several reasons for studying these works. Firstly they are classics, i.e. works of the highest quality which have been very influential on subsequent thought and still have freshness and originality, so that re-reading them suggests new ideas or insights even to experienced philosophers. Secondly, they are formulations of certain well-known attempts to deal with philosophical questions. If one tries to tackle these questions from the beginning on one's own, one may struggle through to an answer, but almost certainly it will be one which has been put forward more plausibly by some past philosopher and has been examined and perhaps refuted by an opponent. In this respect the attempt to do philosophy without having studied earlier philosophers is a bit like trying to play chess without knowing the standard openings. Also, there is good mental training to be found from set books, i.e. in learning to follow a complex line of thought, in seeking how it is developed and justified, what its weaknesses are and so on; the precision and care required to do this properly are well worth cultivating. On the other hand these are *set* books, i.e. theses for examination, criticism and interpretation which are not final but which can be challenged and perhaps superseded. In this they differ from the *text*books of science which provide summaries of facts and an account of what is known. Outside logic there are no distinctively philosophical facts, apart from facts about theories and counter-theories that have been put forward (these may indeed be given in an introductory textbook); the emphasis is all on interpretation and explanation of items of common knowledge or scientific discovery, and on solving the problems to which they give rise.

One qualification should be made to this account of philosophy and its methods. The idea of the philosopher tackling a range of problems, analysing the concepts and presuppositions involved in each, and seeking without preconception or prior commitment the most convincing solution, is a peculiar characteristic of current British and American philosophy. Sixty years ago forms of Idealism similar to Hegel's were dominant; thirty years ago there was a good deal of support for *Logical Positivism,* an extreme form of Empiricism which would accept only logic, mathematics and statements verifiable by science or observation, and which dismissed religion and metaphysics as meaningless. But this modern idea is based on mistrust of all-embracing formulae or 'world views' as a kind of Procrustean bed into which all the facts are forced to fit and as hiding errors beneath pretentious and unanalysed terminology. On the other hand, it invites in return the accusation that its piecemeal treatment may cloak inconsistencies and that its innocent approach to problems in fact conceals an empiricist prejudice (or world view even) which remains uncriticised because not explicit. We can hardly attempt the evaluation of this criticism, but should say that in much Continental philosophy there is an emphasis on system building, on seeking and propagating some very general theory which will provide solutions to all problems and interpretations of all phenomena. Marxism is a widely known example, but the system that is most striking and still influential is the formidable one of Hegel. The Continental philosophy perhaps most frequently mentioned in this country, however, is Existentialism. Paradoxically it is not very systematic and embraces a wide variety of views, but it differs from Anglo-American philosophy in offering dramatically stated formulae as the key to the understanding of man's position and to the conduct of life: for example, 'existence is absurd' (i.e. there is no ultimate rational explanation of life), 'existence precedes essence' (i.e., on Sartre's interpretation, there is no divine blueprint of man, he is what he makes himself and so has free choice, with the 'anguish' or sense of responsibility that this brings). This emphasis on the human predicament of choice and responsibility, which seemed particularly apposite in the dilemma of the French attitude to the German occupation in the Second World War, has meant that except, to some extent, in the field of ethics, Existentialism has aroused much more interest in literary and theological circles in this country than in philosophical ones, which tend to dismiss its basic concepts as not properly analysed.

You should now be ready to tackle the more detailed consideration of typical philosophical problems in the rest of the book. From the nature of the subject-matter some of the discussion inevitably demands an effort from the reader. We should not be giving a fair picture of philosophy if this were not so, but we hope that nevertheless the treatment will be intelligible and that the typical problems raised and the ideas put forward will not only illustrate philosophy but also convey its fascination.

2

Logic and Epistemology

D. R. Bell

Logic as a Science

In one sense, beginning logic in a university course is impossible. The reason is simply that anyone who arrives at a University fit to enter any course is able to do so partly because he has already displayed some minimal skill in constructing, understanding and assessing arguments. The most obvious instance of this in pre-university education is mathematics. Most readers of this book will have carried home with them at some time or other sheets of paper bearing the forbidding 'Given', followed up by 'To Prove'. Even at the most elementary levels of geometrical education one is called upon to construct proofs of certain statements on the basis of others, and this is a logical task. Even if one looks up the proof in a textbook and follows it out, one is deploying logical acumen and setting to work logical distinctions. One is not only doing this, however, in the rarefied atmosphere of the mathematics classroom. When Hamlet poses the question, 'To be or not to be?', and follows it up with seductively poetic consideration of the problem of whether to commit suicide or not, then to understand Hamlet's speech is to understand the arguments he brings to bear on the alternatives which face him.

These examples should be enough to indicate the sense of my opening paradox. You should be able to think of hosts of other examples of arguments which you have come across or produced yourself. Indeed, there is even a case for saying that arguing (by which I do not only mean verbal debate engaged in to win: Hamlet argues with himself) is so common that we do not notice we are doing it; it is rather like breathing in this respect. However, to have spent some part of one's life producing and digesting arguments is not necessarily ever to have considered in a systematic way what one is doing when arguing. It is here that logic as a body of knowledge as well as a practical discipline comes in. The sense then in which one *may* begin logic at the university is that in which one will systematically consider what is involved in doing something one has done before but perhaps never much thought about.

Having said this, it will be convenient to clear out of the way one widespread misconception about the purpose and results of a systematic study of argument. This is that one will argue well if, and only if, one has studied logic. Unfortunately people can go reasonably successfully through logic courses and still argue badly, for it is one thing to know the rules of good argument but quite another thing to deploy them successfully in the conduct of arguments. (It is rather like the difference between knowing the rules of chess, which can be taught fairly quickly to anyone of reasonable intelligence, and winning games by the creation of brilliant mating combinations.) Conversely, someone may tie his opponent in argumentative knots without ever realising the general principles to which he adheres in his verbal knot-tying. On the other hand, forewarned is forearmed, and the study of logic as a systematic science will acquaint a student with the principles of valid arguments and make him sensitive to infringements of them. In fact logic as a science stands to actual arguing much as trigonometry stands to the practical art of bridge-building or arithmetic stands to accountancy. As the statement of the principles of argument, it can both be developed as a theory for its own sake and put to use in the analysis and construction of actual arguments. University courses tend to concentrate on logic as a pure science rather than on its practical applications, and so in this chapter we shall consider some of the basic ideas of logical theory.

First, though, a word about the history of the subject. Systematic reflection upon arguments with a view to eliciting and setting down the principles upon which good arguments

depend, clearly postdates actual argument. The real founder of logic as a science was Aristotle (384–322 B.C.) who codified a type of argument called *syllogism* which he considered of great importance in the construction and exposition of any systematic body of knowledge. His influence upon the subject has been so great that for many people the term 'logic' is associated mainly with Aristotelian syllogistic. There is today no excuse for this. Syllogism is only one kind of argument, as Aristotle himself knew. Since his time and especially in the last century or so, logicians have noticed and systematised other forms of argument. Indeed, following on the suggestions of Leibniz (1646–1716) and through the work of logicians such as Frege (1848–1925), Bertrand Russell and George Boole (1815–1864) we stand today in possession of a single, comprehensive theory of argument which includes the syllogism as just one of its parts. In the formulation of this comprehensive theory much was made possible by consciously resorting to an artificial, symbolic language free from some of the confusing ambiguities of so-called natural languages. To many people there is something daunting about the use of symbols: perhaps it reminds them of mathematics their efforts at which in school met with little reward. But the use of symbols should not put anyone off logic altogether. The basic symbols are easily enough understood when properly explained, and the amount of calculation that one is required to perform with them in any undergraduate logic course is negligible and certainly no more difficult than algebra.

The General Nature of Argument

Logic, we have said, is the systematic science of the principles of arguments. To understand this fully we have to understand what an argument is. Arguing, we have seen, is an activity, something that people do. Arguments are its products, and like all products of activity from motor cars to mousetraps, they are made up of parts. Their parts are *statements*, or *propositions* as they are often called in logic books. So to understand what an argument is we must have some idea of what a statement is. We might first of all think of a statement as a string of sounds or marks on paper (or, for that matter, magnetised particles on plastic tape). But reflection shows that this would be wrong in two ways. First, a random meaningless string of sounds cannot be a statement—they must make up a sentence. Secondly, if one person, for example, says, 'Le ciel est bleu' and another says, 'The sky is blue', then we should certainly want to say that these persons are making the same statement in different strings of sounds. So if we want to say, as we in fact do, that they are both making the same statement, we must abandon any idea of a statement which identifies it even with a meaningful series of marks or sounds. At the very least we shall have to say that a statement is what is expressed by a meaningful series of marks or sounds—or, more exactly, what is expressed by a sentence. Often in order to discuss a statement one must write or utter one of the sentences which expresses it, but this should not tempt one to confuse statement and sentence.

This is a start in the right direction, and it is worth noting in passing that this provisional definition leads on, by the persistent questioning so typical of philosophy, to the question: what is it that makes a series of marks or sounds meaningful? A whole branch of logical theory is concerned with the attempt to say what the meaning of 'meaning' is. It is obvious on reflection, however, that statements are not the only things expressed by sentences. There are, for example, ejaculations, questions and commands. If someone next to me at a football match shouts, 'Come on, United!' I understand him only too well. But what he says is not the sort of thing that one would incorporate in an argument. The reason for this is not far to seek: our spectator's utterance, though perfectly intelligible, is not an utterance which we would consider capable of being true or false. This is the vital point: of the things expressed by sentences statements are those which it makes sense to describe as true or false.

This characterisation of a statement leads us on to a notion of central importance in logic. A few paragraphs back, we rejected the view that a statement might be just the marks or sounds which express it, because it led to a repugnant conclusion, something we refused to believe, namely that the words, 'Le ciel est bleu' do not express the same statement as the words, 'The sky is blue'. Now the two things to get hold of here are firstly, that the view we were considering *implied* this conclusion and secondly, that this implied conclusion was repugnant to us because it was thought false. We could set out the situation schematically in this way:

Stage I	OV	(Original view)
	↓	
	RC	(Repugnant conclusion)
Stage II	~~RC~~	(Struck out because false)
Stage III	~~OV~~	(Struck out because it implies something false).

Notice here how the 'striking out' of RC in stage II has, as a consequence of what is depicted in stage I, the striking out of OV in stage III. What this example brings out is that 'striking out' statements because they are false (and what better reason could one have than this?) has consequences for other statements connected with the struck out statement in special ways, in our example by way of the *implication* depicted in stage I. The falsehood of RC infected OV because OV *implied* RC. So the general lesson to be drawn from this is that statements can be related in such a way that the falsehood and consequent rejection of one statement means that we also have to reject other statements. We trace, so to speak, how the disease of falsehood in one part of the system infects other parts of the system.

One thing this metaphor suggests is that in arguments we can trace not only consequences of the diseased state of falsehood in a collection of statements, but also the consequences of the healthy state of truth. To get back to our example: we ended up rejecting OV, which shows we were not prepared to defend it at all costs, particularly at the cost of maintaining that RC, which it implied, was true. But had we been utterly convinced that OV was true, then we should have been committed to the truth of RC, given the relation depicted in stage I. In general, we may say that just as falsehood in a statement affects the truth or falsity of other statements, then so does the truth of a statement. This means that we can trace the consequences of presumed truths in the hope of establishing yet more truths. Our hope in this direction is, so to speak, to get new truths 'for free', by tracing out the consequences of old ones rather than by direct observation of facts. Deducing new truths from old ones has always been a seductive ideal of scientific method, and it is found in its clearest form in pure mathematics. This ideal of method has been characteristic of that style of philosophy called *rationalism* (see p. 42 below).

To sum up then:

(i) an argument consists of statements, i.e. meaningful symbols which can be true or false;

(ii) these statements may be severally related in such a way that we can trace out in the related statements the consequences in point of truth or falsity of truth or falsity in a given statement.

(iii) The interest of this is mainly twofold. We may be interested either in adjustments which have to be made as a consequence of eliminating erroneous statements, or in using truths already on hand to establish other truths.

One final point concerning (iii) above. It is obvious enough that carrying out the procedures described there presupposes that we are already in possession of some truths, that, in short, we need a starting-point. This is most obvious with regard to using truths to generate new truths. However, it is equally true of the procedures whereby we eliminate falsehoods. Knowing that some statement is false amounts to knowing the truth of the statement which denies it. For example, knowing the falsehood of 'Today is Tuesday' amounts to knowing the truth of 'It is not the case that today is Tuesday'. The observation that we need already to possess truths to get logic going at all was made long ago by Aristotle. It has the very important consequence that if one already needs to know some true statements to get logic going in the first place, then not everything which is known to be true is established by logical procedures alone. Hence the need for that branch of philosophy called epistemology (or theory of knowledge) which investigates what can be known to be true and how. This fundamental enquiry, for the reason just stated, must go beyond the merely logical. We shall deal with its problems and approaches in the second part of this chapter (pp. 39 ff—those impatient with logical analyses may proceed straight to that point).

Steps towards the analysis of arguments

Whether logic is studied as a systematic science or for its practical applications, the analysis of arguments is important. In this section we consider some of the basic ideas which underlie any such analysis.

In analysing a particular argument one must first identify the component statements of it. This preliminary stage can cause a surprising amount of trouble because a single sentence is not always, for logical purposes, to be identified with a single statement. For example, 'John and Joan ran a mile' is one sentence but two statements, namely 'John ran a mile' and 'Joan ran a mile', asserted together. This example is worth dwelling upon, for it could be argued that 'John and Joan ran a mile' has as much right to be considered one statement as 'John ran a mile'. However, the point is this: 'John ran a mile' cannot be broken down into parts that are statements; it is what we may call a basic statement.

Next we must consider some of the ways in which these basic statements are combined or transformed. The example we dealt with a moment ago shows that one way in which complex statements are formed from simple ones is by means of 'and'. Another familiar one is by use of 'or', though we must be careful to know whether its use is exclusive, e.g. 'his book is on the table or on the desk', where one of the simple statements must be false, or inclusive, where both of the simple statements may be true, e.g. 'These plants cannot stand frost or drought' (nor can they stand both frost and drought). One may also make statements out of statements *without* combining two or more statements together. Recollect that to say we know a statement to be false comes to the same thing as saying we know the truth of its denial or, as logicians usually say, its *negation*. Hence, to put 'not' into a statement is to make a different statement out of that statement, indeed one is inclined to add a *very* different statement. Consider, for example, the difference between 'My best friend is an expert thief' to 'My best friend is *not* an expert thief'. The point is that the second statement is different from the first not because it consists of the first statement together with another statement: rather we have modified a statement to produce a different statement. These may seem trivial examples, but like geometry and other branches of mathematics, logic is built upon simple foundations. More important, these examples introduce us to the idea of words in a language like 'and', 'not' and 'or', which are of *logical* or *formal* significance and play a vital part in arguments. The logical or formal resources of a language are being exploited all the time by language users, and logic as a science must isolate and codify them.

Let us move on then to another example, central to logic, of a formal linguistic device. Recall once more our specimen argument, p. 21; recollect how, in its diagram form, we used an arrow in order to represent one statement *following from* another or, what would appear to amount to the same thing, one statement *implying* another. This group of notions 'implication', 'following from', 'consequence of', 'deducible from' are usually indicated in English by the words, 'if . . ., then . . .', where the blanks can be filled in by statements (or 'if . . ., . . .', the word 'then' being understood; for clarity 'then' is never omitted in this expression in logic). So we can say that 'If . . ., then . . .' relates two statements but not in the same way as 'and'. In what way then, does it relate the statements? At this point we need to recall what was said above about tracing the consequences in a set of statements of the truth and falsity of various particular statements in that set. The truth or falsity of any single statement only infects other statements because the statements in question are logically related to each other. Thus if the statement:

(1): All introductory logic courses are difficult,

is logically related to the statement:

(2): This introductory logic course is difficult,

then the truth or falsity of the one statement will be affected by the truth or falsity of the other. Our task now is to see precisely how this happens in the case of 'If . . ., then . . .'.

Now one thing about this way of making complex statements out of simpler ones is clear: that it can be used to formulate the idea of going from one statement to another that is involved in argument. For example, we could put (1) and (2) above into the 'If . . ., then . . .' framework in order to make it clear that if we have got (1) as a truth, then we are entitled to assert (2) because, as is said, (2) follows from (1), or, alternatively (1) implies (2). That we do this, in effect, to give notice that the relation indicated by the form of statement composition in question here is a *truth-preserving* relationship. As mentioned earlier we have an interest in truth-preserving relations between statements because one motive of logical investigation is that of using truths already acquired to acquire new truth. To do this we need to be supplied not only with true starting-points but also with statements that license the passage from one truth to another. This is the (or, more properly, one) function of the 'If . . ., then . . .' form of statement composition.

A corollary, i.e. further consequence, of all this is that the one case ruled out by the 'If . . ., then . . .' way of joining statements is the case where we should be proceeding from a truth to a falsehood. (If this were allowed, then it would be difficult to see what point there would be in investigating the consequences of acquired truths at all, for we should be as likely to end up with falsehoods as with truths.) In other words, the 'If . . ., then . . .' type of relation relates two statements or, to use the jargon, 'holds between' them, in every case except that in which the statement following the 'if' (called the *antecedent*) is true, and the statement following the 'then' (called the *consequent*) is false. To make this clearer let us investigate other possibilities, with examples. Obviously enough the condition just laid down doesn't apply to cases where the antecedent is false, for it mentions only cases of true antecedents. So if we start with the false statements:

(3): This man is twenty-one feet tall,

we could (and indeed might) proceed either to the equally false statement:

(4): This man is at least nineteen feet tall,

or to the true statement:

(5): This man is at least three feet tall.

What these examples bring out is that it is possible, though not in general desirable, to get truths from falsehoods and that the reason it is not in general desirable to proceed in this fashion is that one is just as likely to end up with falsehoods.

The relation of implication which I have been explaining is generally called by logicians *material implication*. It represents the *minimum* conditions that must hold if one statement is to be said to follow logically from another. It is of the utmost importance to grasp the point that the conditions are minimal. We can bring this out by considering a question that should have cropped up already in the mind of the reader, namely: How do we know when we are justified in joining a pair of statements by the 'if . . ., then . . .' locution? Surely, if the account just given is sound, we can do this with any two statements, provided that either the antecedent is false or the consequent is true. For example, we can say:

(6): If Glasgow is the largest city in the world, then two is an even number.

Yet no one would even think of proceeding from the antecedent of (6) to its consequent, indeed, nobody could. What this brings out is that normally we only put forward statements of implication when there is some connexion between the component statements other than that minimal connexion demanded by material implication. For example, the connexion between:

(1): All introductory courses are difficult

and

(2): This introductory logic course is difficult

is obvious, for it depends upon what is true of each and every introductory logic course being true of any particular logic course. However, to recognise connexions of this kind is not inconsistent with our minimal condition. Indeed, in one way it illustrates our minimal condition for, in the example just given, the understanding of the connexion guarantees the transmission of truth from (1) to (2). In general, we can say that material implication is the basic logical relation because it guarantees the transmission of truth from one statement to another, independently of the kind of connexion holding between the statements concerned.

At this point it will be convenient to introduce a distinction between argument and implication. It has already been stated that implication is fundamental to an argument. But acute readers will have already noticed that to put forward implications which meet the minimal conditions of material implication is not to argue. A person who asserts:

(7): If the Prime Minister sacks half his Cabinet, then he weakens his own position,

may have said something that is true. But merely doing this is not arguing. In order to argue one has to draw a conclusion from certain other statements, usually called *premisses*. Now while (7) could figure as either a premiss or a conclusion in an argument, expressing a connexion between two component statements, this in turn means that it does not by itself express an argument. For an argument requires both premiss(es) and conclusion. We can bring this out in other ways as well. (7), which by now ought to be recognised as an implication, is sometimes called by logicians a *conditional* statement. This is because it only says that one thing is so, *given* that another is so. (Contrast a *categorical* statement which asserts something unconditionally.) But it does not say that this other is so; it in no way states or implies that the Prime Minister has sacked half his Cabinet. However, given that we have a ground for asserting that the Prime Minister has sacked half his Cabinet, we could use (7) with a further premiss in order to draw the conclusion that he has weakened his own position. Set out the argument would look like this:

(7): If the Prime Minister sacks half his Cabinet, then he weakens his own position.

(8): He has done so.

(Notice that (8) expresses a colloquial assertion of the first component of (7), a point to be watched in reducing samples of arguments to logical form.)

(9): Therefore, he has weakened his own position.

Now we easily think of the statements (7), (8) and (9) as two asserted premisses and one drawn conclusion. That a conclusion is drawn we know because of the typical mark, explicit in this case, 'therefore'. Other similar conclusion indicators are 'Hence', 'In consequence', 'So', 'It follows that', 'I conclude that'. This contrasts with any statement of an implication which, as we have seen, is always conditional despite the fact that, as stating a logical connexion, it is categorical. To make this clearer, consider the statement,

(10): If all men are twenty feet tall, then all men are at least ten feet tall.

As expressing a relation of implication between two statements this example is categorical and makes a definite, and in this case true, claim. But the definite claim, what is categorically asserted, is neither the statement that all men are twenty feet tall nor that all men are at least ten feet tall. These statements, as they occur in the example, are not asserted. It would in any case be absurd to assert them for we know them both to be false. But it is not absurd to assert what the example as a whole asserts, namely the implication holding between its two components. Sometimes the distinction between an argument and an implication is put by saying that arguing is something people do, possibly a psychological or verbal activity, while implication is not an activity but a logical relation. There is an element of truth in this that our analysis brings out: one does not have an argument unless a conclusion has been drawn whereas one can state implications without drawing any conclusions.

Nevertheless, the relationship between implication and argument is more intimate than leaving things here would suggest. For we can say that every argument is associated with an implication in so far as we can restate every argument by putting all the premisses in the antecedent of a conditional assertion and putting the conclusion as the consequent. Thus to reform (7), (8), (9), in this way:

(11): If (if the Prime Minister sacks half his Cabinet, then he weakens his own position) *and* he has done so, then he has weakened his own position.

This looks a little queer and complicated. Certainly, we have no argument here, for no conclusion is drawn. Still, we do have a statement of the implication that lies behind the argument consisting of (7), (8) and (9). But we must not understand this as meaning that anyone who argues as in (7), (8), (9) has in mind (11) as the principle of their argument. (11) is a reconstruction for logico-theoretical purposes of the principle of the argument (7), (8), (9). (This principle (11), or rather a generalised form of it, is usually called in logic books, the principle of affirming the antecedent of a conditional.)

We are now in a position to say something further about the nature of logic as the systematic study of argument. A large part of logic will be related to people's actual arguments much as (11) is related to (7), (8), (9), but will present such principles of argument in a more generalised way. The generalisation will consist in dropping out of the principle stated any *content* that might be involved in an argument to which the principle applied and retaining only its *form*. The dropping out of content here is analogous to something one is familiar with from elementary algebra when one replaces numbers with letters. For example, the principle (11) above contains references to a Cabinet and a Prime Minister but these references are not part of the form of the statement. If we drop them out and replace the constituent statements by letters (sometimes called *variables*) we get:

(12): If (if p, then q) and p, then q.

The notion of a variable is important in modern logic and complicated. The p's and q's of this example are really to be regarded as schematic letters, standing in for any statement expression that might be placed where the schematic letters are, subject to the restriction that wherever p occurs the same statement is put, wherever q . . . etc.

We can say, then, that in logic we try to systematise and present the *formal* principles of statement connexion that are employed in argument. This formulation makes clear why one has to be alive to the various words in a language that are indicative of formal connexion like those we have met already viz. *and*, *or* and *if . . . , then. . . .* These words are our clue in any actual case to the logical form of a statement.

In order to clarify what has been said still further I am now going to extend our stock of logical words. So far we have dealt with logical words that join statements together. However, it is important to notice that there are also formal words that occur within statements and in virtue of which we can say that statements are logically related in a sense stronger than that implied by the connexion of material implication. Consider the statements:

(13): All students of logic are quick-witted.

(14): No student of logic is quick-witted.

A little thought about (13) and (14) reveals that both of them cannot be true. One way of putting this would be to say, using our 'if . . , then . . .' way of connecting statements:

(15): If (13), then not (14), *and* if (14), then not (13).

Furthermore, we are justified in saying this because of the nature of (13) and (14). (13) contains the word 'All', which makes it clear that something is being asserted of each and every logic student. (14), while not containing the word 'all', nevertheless makes clear that something, the same thing as in (13), is being denied of every logic student. Hence, the justification for (15), as you can verify for yourselves. Note carefully that (14) succeeded in denying something of each and every member of a group without the word 'all'—which we could call the generality word *par excellence*—being used at all. Thus in order to classify a statement correctly for logical purposes we cannot always rely on there being explicit indicators, or even trust implicitly the indicators there are, cf. 'or' p. 23. For example,

(16): John Doe is quick-witted

is anything but a universal or general statement, and the clue to the character as a *singular* statement lies in our understanding of what the expression 'John Doe' is. In grammar we call it a 'proper name' and understand by this that it is used to refer to an individual. Proper names are not the only words with this function of singular reference. Words like 'this' and 'that' work in a singular way as well. Consider also:

(17): The man who broke the bank at Monte Carlo is quick-witted.

Here we use a descriptive phrase ('the man . . . Monte Carlo') in order to pick out a particular person.

Without going too deeply into these complexities, it is possible to grasp the fact that the generality or singularity of statements can have a bearing on the logical relations between them. It was this aspect of logic that first received systematic formulation in Aristotle's account of syllogistic reasoning. A syllogism is an argument consisting of three statements, two of which are premisses and the other of which is the conclusion. The logical relations in virtue of which the conclusion may be said to follow from the premisses depend upon the characteristics of the three statements as universal, singular or particular, and negative or affirmative. ('Particular' is the technical term for statements about at least one of a group, e.g. 'some students are tall'. Note that 'some' in the logical sense of 'at least one' differs slightly from the ordinary sense of the word. Unfortunately in inductive logic 'particular' is used simply as the opposite of 'general' or 'universal', and so covers both singular and particular in the narrow sense. We shall use this wider sense from p. 35 on.) Thus, to take a traditional example, in the syllogism:

(18): All men are mortal,
Socrates is a man,
Therefore, Socrates is mortal.

we have respectively a universal affirmative premiss, a singular affirmative premiss, and a singular affirmative conclusion. Nowadays in the comprehensive theory of logical argument, syllogistic reasoning and the principles of it elicited by Aristotle form just a part, although an important part, of general logic. One reason for this importance is that syllogism always operates with at least one universal premiss and such premisses are difficult to come by. We shall return to this topic in the discussion of inductive reasoning.

Enough has been indicated of the scope and nature of logical enquiry for the reader to follow, if he has not already thought out for himself, a sceptical line of argument about the uses of logic as considered so far. It might be argued that even though logic places at our disposal a battery of tests for telling whether a conclusion follows from a given set of premisses, it is still pretty useless as a means of obtaining truths. For even if we know that a set of premisses *S* implies a conclusion *C*, we cannot know whether or not *C* is true unless we know that the set *S* consists of true statements. One possible reply to this would be to say that we could derive *S* as conclusions from other premisses, call them S^1. However, it is obvious that this will simply raise the same difficulty again. So we are justified in saying, as Aristotle said long ago, that logic is useless unless there is some way of getting hold of true statements independently of logic. However, even if this could not be done, it might be said that logic does have a limited use. It enables us, so to speak, to arrange our ignorance; for, as we have seen, there can be logical relations between false as well as true statements. Still even this limited view might not make logic immune from sceptical doubts, for systematic logic itself purports to consist of true principles. (It is often said that the most important of them are self-evidently true, notably the so-called 'laws of thought' of which an example is the principle that every statement is either true or false.) While the sceptical possibility that we do not know anything to be true remains undisposed of, logic falls under the shadow of scepticism as much as anything else.

Form and content: The Transition to Epistemology

The point touched upon at the end of the previous section serves to press us in the direction of widening our enquiry. We began with the idea that logic was the systematic study of argument. Arguments, we noted, consist of statements, true or false, which are logically related. We further noted the diversity of these relations and also the possibility of a systematic and exact statement of the principles governing the employment of these relations in statement composition and in argument. However, the need for premisses which are known to be true and which are not simply derived logically from other premisses concerning which the same question could arise, points to an incompleteness in logic as we have treated it so far. Some terminological preliminaries will help to clarify the situation.

We have already introduced the idea of logical relations between statements being dependent upon the *formal* characteristics of those statements rather than upon their *content*. We noted, moreover, a number of words that appear to have the role of indicating formal status. It is this that lies behind the idea of logic as *formal logic*. Other terms which are used in a similar way are *deductive logic* and *symbolic logic*. This last is interesting for it is due an extension of those possibilities or generalisation that we touched upon in the treatment of (13), (14) and (15). Instead of using English words like 'If . . ., then . . .' in (15) we could have used a symbol to denote this relation, say '$\rightarrow$' or '$\supset$'. In this way one can conveniently symbolise and interrelate all the principles of formal relations between statements. Thus we get a strong tendency in modern logic to equate the term 'symbolic logic' with the terms 'formal logic' and 'deductive logic'.

On this use, however, symbolic logic will have to do only with the form of statements and not with their content. And if we are seeking a way of establishing statements without deriving them deductively from other statements, then we need to find a way of establishing the *content* as well as the *form* of statements. As far as establishing general statements is concerned we are taken into the sphere of another kind of logic from that which we have been considering so far. This kind of logic sometimes goes by the name of *inductive logic* in order to contrast it as clearly as possible with purely formal deductive logic.

(In terms of the foregoing argument, it would be better to

consider this branch of philosophy, namely the problem of establishing universal premisses independently of formal considerations, under the title of epistemology (cf. p. 39). For the epistemological question of how we can arrive, independently of deductive logic, at statements known to be true, is a more general way of putting the essential problem that faces inductive logic. But to avoid causing difficulties for you in further reading we shall be more conventional and start with the problem of inductive logic as it is commonly conceived, namely as a means of inferring general or universal statements from a set of statements which, severally, are neither general nor universal. Here we shall find a clear contrast with deductive logic that will lead us into epistemology.)

The Problem of Inductive Logic

At (18) we considered an example of a deductive argument involving a universal and a singular premiss. From them we were able in virtue of their form to derive a singular conclusion deductively. We needed both these premisses to derive the conclusion. Equally, we would need to know that both these premisses are true in order to establish the conclusion as true. It is in general the case that where a syllogism is concerned we need at least one universal premiss. The reason for this can be seen when we reflect that in order to go from one individual fact to another, from say:

Socrates is a man,

to:

Socrates is mortal,

we need to establish some general connexion between a man and being mortal. This is done for us by the universal premiss of (18) which really says that if anything is a man, then it is mortal. This naturally raises the question of how general premisses can be established non-deductively; how, for example, we can establish the following:

All men are mortal.
All iron expands when heated.
All swans are white.
Prime Ministers who swing the axe get off-balance.
All light passing from one transparent medium to another is refracted.

As some of these examples indicate, our question also concerns the activities of the natural scientist. It is not unusual to think of him as attempting by his experiments to establish general laws, albeit in mathematical form. Newton saw this very well when he established it as a principle of natural philosophy—what nowadays we call physics—that fire burns in Australia as well as in England. Knowing a general truth relieves one of the necessity of examining particular cases. Also one can employ it in advance of experience to *predict* the properties of this or that. So our question is important—indeed it constitutes the central question of the philosophy of science, although the simplicity of the question often gets lost amongst the complexities of the answers given to it.

The most natural approach to the problem is to say that we arrive at general truths by examining particular cases. One might even suggest that this is the role of experiment and observation in natural science. One examines this swan, that swan; one gathers authenticated reports from all over the civilised world to the effect that all examined swans are white; then one simply concludes that all swans are white. But what sort of concluding is this? One is not, as in a deductive argument, going from a statement about all things of a certain kind to statements of about one or some of these things. What we are after is something that goes completely in the opposite direction, something moreover that on the principles of *deductive* reasoning is fallacious—a premiss about all *examined* swans, being only about *some* swans and not all, does not entitle one to a conclusion about *all* swans.

At this point a tough-minded person might be inclined to give up altogether hope of answering the question and conclude that the gap yawning between 'some' and 'all' is unbridgable. But one should note that this profoundly sceptical move really amounts to giving up all attempt to validate general laws in science by reference to particular cases. Rather than do that, many philosophers have tried to define a relationship between general statements and particular cases which would in some way validate non-deductively the passage from 'some' to 'all'.

One common way of dealing with the problem has been to make the number of particular instances examined count towards the validation of a general law. This we might call the way of probability. For example, if we have examined hundreds and hundreds of swans and have found that they are all white and we have discovered no cases of black swans, then we are justified in saying that it is highly probable that all swans are white. The trouble with this sort of approach is that it avoids the issue. For what we wish to validate is not a statement to the effect that it is highly probable that all swans are white, but rather one to the effect that all swans are white. In other words this approach replaces the gap between 'some' and 'all' with an equally unbridgable gap between 'It is highly probable that . . .' and 'It is the case that . . .'.

Another approach to the problem is the suggestion that in the examination of *one* case something can be discovered which validates the general law. We might in practice need to examine several cases before we see the validation; but that is a matter of lack of insight in our part—the conclusion will not depend on the number of cases. Suppose the generalisation whose validation is at issue is the statement that all events of type *A* cause events of type *B*. The present suggestion is that in examining a single instance of an *A* event causing a *B* event, we find that if *A* happens *B* must happen, cannot but happen, i.e. we come across a link or connexion between the two which guarantees that any other event of an *A*-type will be similarly related to one of a *B*-type. In short, if we can discover what philosophers call a *necessary connexion* between events, then the discovery of one such connexion is all we require to validate a law relating to all events of the kind in question.

Someone putting forward this type of view is likely to have in mind a mathematical analogy. Sometimes in elementary geometry we consider a single diagram or figure and come to see by inspection and explanation the truth of the generalisation, e.g. that in all isosceles triangles the angles at the base are equal. It seems that here we have a case of basing the true generalisation on one examined instance; there is clearly a necessary connexion between equality of sides and equality of angles so that the one cannot occur without the other.

The claim then is that we should try to find in the data from which we make our inductive generalisations, some necessary connexion which ensures their truth. In the case of 'all iron expands on heating' for example, we must find something in the heating and the composition of the iron which ensures that the expansion occurs; if it *must* occur then it will occur in every case and our generalisation is justified. Or again, if the generalisation is 'Sitting in a draught when overheated causes one to catch cold' then we want to find something in the cooling effect of the draught which makes catching cold inevitable. In this way, we might hope to close not just the gap between 'some' and 'all' but even the gap between 'one' and 'all'.

But can such necessary connexions between events be discovered? A resounding and, to judge from the subsequent history of the subject, successful negative answer was given to this question by the Scottish philosopher David Hume (1711-76). Basically Hume's justification for his negative answer consisted in two simple observations. The first was that in any case of alleged necessary connexion we never in fact *experience* more than one event following upon another. Though we may subsequently *assume* a necessary connexion, the most to which we can point in our experience as warranting this are the events concerned succeeding one another as closely as they may. We never come across as an item in our experience any necessity sticking events together like glue (cf. p. 123 for another application of this point)—however much we investigate the iron for example we only find that molecular changes *in fact* follow the heating, not that they *must*.

Hume's second and connected observation was that even in cases where we do assume a necessary connexion between events, when, for example, we believe that consumption of a specific quantity of gin produces intoxication, it would not be absurd (though it might as a matter of fact be false) to think of the events turning out other than they have, to suppose that drinking gin does nothing more to one than drinking water. The significance of this is that there is no absurdity involved in thinking of all the causal regularities in which we believe as being different from what in fact they are. This brings out the further point that we believe in the regularities that we do because they are the regularities we have found in our experience. But what we do not find there is anything that corresponds to the necessity of these regularities.

Hume would appear to be correct in both his contentions, and this implies that the road from 'some' to 'all', or from experiments to general laws, does not run *via* necessary connexions as items found in experience. So this solution to our original problem is unsatisfactory. Nevertheless, the problem does remain that we do believe some causal regularities to hold and some scientific generalisations to be true. What grounds, in the light of the abortive solutions proposed, have we for this? One suggestion that is of value is simply to give up the problem in its original form as an irrelevant problem, to stop trying to build a bridge from 'some' to 'all' which will validate universal statements by appeal to particular facts. It is suggested that we take our problem not to be that of *validating* universal statements but rather to be that of *falsifying* such statements by appeal to particular facts. On this sort of view the passage from 'This or that swan is white', to 'All swans are white' is not a logical or even a quasi-logical step. Even though a series of particular observations or experiments may suggest to us a general law, this is of merely psychological interest, for the task of validating the law by reference to the particular cases is like ladling water with a sieve. What is of logical importance on this view is that a general statement or law once formulated and promulgated shall, despite severe testing and systematic attempts to discover counter-instances, nevertheless remain unviolated. In short, the view of scientific laws which emerges from this account (due, in the modern period, to Professor Sir K. R. Popper) is that while we can never know them to be true, we are at least in the happy position of sometimes being able conclusively to prove them to be false.

Paradoxical as this reversal of the inductive problem sounds, it does emphasise the importance in scientific practice of devising systematic tests designed to maximise the chances of falsifying a hypothesis. The ideal scientist appears on this account as a masochist with respect to his most cherished hypotheses; he submits them to the most destructive testing he can devise. These hypotheses are in their turn only worthy of belief if they have survived rigorous and ingenious attempts at falsification.

But whatever value Popper's views may have as a description of scientific method, or even only as a recommendation about it, one is nevertheless left with a feeling of dissatisfaction. We started with the question of how general laws can be validated, i.e. shown to be true on the basis of an examination of the particular cases to which they apply. And yet the answer seems to be that we have found no way of establishing these laws—the most that we can ever know is that some law or generalisation cannot be true; what, particularly, we can never know but can at most believe, is that an unrefuted but systematically tested general statement is true. Hence there is here for many people an unsolved problem of induction. Furthermore these difficulties immediately raise the question of whether there are *any* ways of coming to know things which do not leave one in a similarly unsatisfactory position. To answer this question one has to undertake a general and wholesale investigation of the notion of knowledge itself. This study belongs in philosophy to the general field of *epistemology*, a word whose meaning is 'the science of knowledge'.

Epistemology

We can conveniently begin to expose some of the central

problems of epistemology by pointing out that in our discussion of inductive logic which led us to doubt whether we can ever know any general statement to be true, we nevertheless took it for granted throughout that we did at least know to be true particular statements of the kind exemplified by, 'Socrates is a man', 'This swan is white', 'This iron rail has expanded' and so forth. In the context of a general enquiry into the notion of knowledge, however, we must not stop short of investigating even the modest claims made by particular statements. This is one source of the impatience that many people feel with epistemology. Not everyone is worried by scepticism over the truth of abstruse high-level scientific hypotheses such as the theory of general relativity. Concern with truth at this level can with plausibility be considered a matter of professional gamesmanship in which the relatively incurious are not essentially implicated. But when the philosopher extends his sceptical questioning to mundane items of common knowledge or assumption, and asks whether the paper on which this is printed really exists, or whether it is really the colour it seems to be, then an air of unreality not unsurprisingly begins to creep into the discussion. 'Surely,' one is inclined to say, 'nothing can overturn, or make plausible sceptical questioning of, such ordinary items of knowledge as that I have a body, that I was not born five minutes ago, that I shall at sometime die and so on?' If this is what epistemology is about, then one begins to wonder why any intelligent person should bother with it.

While not entering a full-scale defence of the viability of the epistemological enterprise, one might try as follows to alleviate the air of unreality it often generates. Firstly, it needs to be realised that many highly questionable but, if true, important claims to knowledge have been couched in particular statements as well as generalisations. Probably the most striking of these is the monotheistic basic claim that God exists. So the general question of the varied ways in which we obtain our knowledge of particular matters of fact will cover not just the claims of ordinary life which it seems paradoxical to question, but also particular claims which, on the face of it, have anything but an axiomatic status. If someone claims knowledge of an omniscient, omnipotent, infinite being outside space and time, then this can scarcely be treated as part of the common stock of information possessed by all rational beings.

Secondly, it should be borne in mind that the primary purpose of the epistemologist is not to provide us with instructions for obtaining new items of information. If this were his purpose, then it would indeed be a matter for reproach that epistemologists have spilt so much ink in laying bare grounds for scepticism concerning commonplace matters of belief. The main motive of his enquiry is not practical in this way, however, but springs from a legitimate intellectual curiosity concerning the grounds upon which commonplace matters of belief and knowledge rest. Occasionally, of course, such curiosity is induced in any of us by puzzles and inconsistencies noticed in commonplace beliefs. We are all familiar, for example, with the fact that a stick half in water looks bent when we would claim to know that it is in fact straight. Again, blood seen in a microscope does not look red—what then is its real colour? And the moon near the horizon looks larger than when high in the sky, but it is not nearer at the horizon and it does not change size—indeed its real size is different from all its apparent ones. Reflection upon such anomalies leads obviously to the more general question of how the way things look to us is related to our claim to know what they *really* are. And this kind of question is meat and drink to the philosopher with his concern for fundamental questions of high generality. (Epistemology can sometimes also be attractive to a student in that it affords an array of (often fallacious) arguments with which the unthinking certitudes of parents, schoolteachers and the older generation generally may be confounded.)

All the same, in modern epistemological discussion which began with Descartes, one can find practical motives for undertaking epistemological enquiry lying alongside sheer theoretical curiosity. Descartes begins his *Discourse on Method* (1637) with a series of observations on the unsatisfactory state of the sciences, both human and natural, of his day. He appears to be impressed by the fact that nothing interesting in them seems certain and that they are full of disputes which never appear to be moving towards a solution. Furthermore, it is clear that he believes himself to be in possession of methodological cures for this sorry state of affairs, i.e. he thinks of epistemological investigation as having a practical payoff in terms of the progress and certainty of the special sciences. Descartes' reasons for holding this belief are complex, and a critical assessment of them would be still more complex. One thing is clear, however, namely that his remedies for the uncertainty and obscurity of the sciences are based upon what he took to be the method whereby he had scored his own successes in mathematics. What Descartes sought to do was to generalise the mathematician's emphasis on analysis, clear definition of key terms, and deduction. In so doing he was not only providing an instance of something common in epistemological discussion, namely taking as the model of *all* knowledge ways of knowing specific to a *single* discipline such as mathematics; he was also initiating a great divide in the history of modern epistemology, that between rationalism and empiricism. Briefly—and we shall explain this more fully later—rationalism is the view that rejects sensory experience as a source of truth and holds that only in the intuitions and operations of reason, as in mathematics, is true knowledge obtained; empiricism, in contrast, holds that knowledge is based upon and even derived from sensory experience, and tends to limit pure reason severely as a source of factual knowledge. Note however that what are broadly classified as rationalist and empiricist philosophical systems often contain elements of both standpoints. Any serious comprehensive philosopher is too well attuned to the difficulties of his undertaking to brush aside lightly the difficulties raised by his adopted starting-point. The problems left unsolved by empiricism may often appear to find solution in the rationalist framework and vice versa. Also attempts have been made, of which Kant's is the most notable, to combine the merits of rationalism and empiricism in a single system. We shall now turn to one aspect of this dichotomy as an illustration of epistemological discussion.

Rationalism and Empiricism: The Basis of Knowledge

You will remember that in the last section the point was made that in the search for true premisses the inductivist philosopher was interested mainly in justifying general statements on the basis of particular observations. He does not raise the question of whether we have any true particular statements to underpin general conclusions. In justification of this he might say that it is carrying sceptical enquiry too far to suggest that particular observations of material bodies expressed in statements such as, 'The water boiled at 100°C', 'The litmus paper, on entering the liquid, turned red', 'The tracks of the particles intersected at 85°', need to be grounded in the way that general statements do; for such statements qualify as *observation statements,* that is they are grounded simply upon particular seeings, smellings, feelings, etc. Stated more theoretically, he would be resting his case for the certitude of observation statements upon the empiricist view that sense-experience and sense-perception afford us access to and knowledge of a world of particular realities and their properties. It is this view, incontestable as it may at first seem, which we shall now examine in the spirit of the generalised and radical questioning of epistemology.

A number of assumptions lie hidden in this general empiricist position. The most important is that there exists a world of independent realities, independent that is of those perceivers who, it is claimed, learn truths about this world by experiencing it. What it is important to notice about this assumption is that its validation appears to rest upon experience which, at the very minimum, means that the perceiver is related at least sometimes to this independent world. So this world cannot be wholly independent of the perceiver who claims knowledge of it; this perceiver must at least stand to this world in the general relation which we can term 'having sense-experience of this world'. It is this relation which needs to be clarified for a full understanding of the position. The usual account given of this relationship is as follows: perceivers are equipped with senses—sight, touch, hearing, etc.—which are activated by coming into relationship with independent bodies. This activation of a sense or senses by a body or bodies is a necessary condition of any experiencing of the world at all. *A* is a necessary condition of *B* if *B* never happens (or never could happen) without *A*. So the general empiricist position appears to rest upon the view that experiences are *caused* in us by objects acting upon our senses.

This picture of experiencing the world fits in well with certain familiar and less familiar facts. Among familiar observations that fit it are the various cases of sensory deprivation and malfunctioning. The blind man never visually experiences anything in the world; the deaf man never aurally experiences anything and so on. These cases confirm that proper functioning of the appropriate sense is a necessary condition for the production in someone of the appropriate sense experience. Less familiar facts that appear to support the causal picture are those afforded by the physiological study of sensation, which reveals the complex series of electro-chemical effects in the nervous system which result from the stimulation of the sense-organ and upon which sensory experience depends. Furthermore, the eyes and ears themselves are not stimulated by the object perceived but by light or sound waves which come from the object. So perception of the object is not direct and instantaneous, indeed the causal process may take considerable time. One can estimate the distance of a thunderstorm by counting the seconds between the flash and the thunderclap, for the sound travels much more slowly than the light of the flash, even though both started together. But light itself takes time to travel, and the distance of stars is measured in light-years, i.e. by the time light takes to reach us. So if I see a star fifty light-years away, light from it has taken fifty years to reach my eye, and the star itself may have ceased to exist by the time I report its existence on the basis of observation.

In addition to these considerations counting in favour of the causal view, it is worth mentioning two other features of experience which, while not requiring a causal view, nevertheless appear best explained by it.

The first set of phenomena are those which are generally known under the generic title *Relativity of Perception.*

Among them are such familiar facts as that one and the same thing appears differently to observers differently situated with regard to it. Such differences may cover, in vision, an object appearing a different size, shape or colour to two observers, one close to, the other farther away. In the aural field differences of situation with regard to a source of sound may make the difference between hearing a muffled sound or a clear one, a high-pitched sound or a low-pitched one, and so on. An instance is the Doppler effect, viz. a change of pitch in a sound due to the speed, relative to the observer, at which the source of sound is travelling; for example to listeners in a railway station (but not to those on the train) the note of the whistle of an express seems to change in pitch as the train passes through. On the causal theory of the genesis of experience we should expect these differences. Difference of relation between observer and object result in differences of stimulus (light or sound waves) at the sense-organ and so will produce different effects in the observer.

The second set of phenomena have been variously referred to as illusions, hallucinations and even sometimes delusions. The characteristic feature of hallucinations is that we appear to have a case of experience of something without it in fact being the case that what seems to be experienced is there at all. The causal account explains this by saying that effects in the sense-organ or nervous system, which would be caused by an appropriate object if it were present, are in fact caused by disturbances of another kind, normally within the hallucinated person's body. One example is the desert traveller, whose nervous system is affected by dehydration so that he 'sees' a palm-surrounded oasis. Another is the alcoholic with *delirium tremens* who 'sees' pink elephants or snakes. Other examples are the many striking results of stimulation of the brain by electric currents during brain surgery. A patient of Penfield's reported hearing parts of Beethoven's Fifth Symphony as a result of such stimulation.

Finally, before leaving facts which seem to support and be made intelligible by the causal theory, we ought to mention these features of experience which suggest that in experience something not ourselves seems to be doing something to us, to be acting upon us. One can actually feel assaulted by say, a bright flash, a clap of thunder or sudden excessive heat. In virtue of such experiences we are inclined to think that in all experience whatsoever something is being done to us. So strong is the hold of this picture of the observer beleaguered by sensory stimuli at, so to speak, the weak spots in his armour, that we tend to forget how much of our experience of the world is a calm and pointless passage of appearings and sensings. Many philosophers of perception, at least as far back as Plato, have tended to assimilate the effect of the external world upon us to the case of the signet ring's impression on the wax. Hume even called perceptions *impressions,* while at the same time warning his readers that he did not use this term to connote the manner whereby we came by these perceptions. Be that as it may it is now time to examine more critically the picture of experience presented by the causal theory.

We said at the outset of this discussion that the causal theory of perception is, in part, an attempt at interpreting the relation between a perceiver and his world that is presupposed by the general empiricist position. The first critical remark to be made about this interpretation is that it complicates the relation between perceiver and perceived in a way that has no warrant from experience itself. It suggests that between the object perceived and our perceiving of it, there exists a complicated chain of events. Now it is certainly the case that in no act of perception is any perceiver directly aware of these events in all their complexity. Indeed, it might be argued that no perceiver could be. For what the theory does is to explain any given experience as an effect of something else. So we cannot equate any single experience with the cause of this effect, for it is essential to the significance of any causal statement that the cause and effect to which it refers should be distinct from each other. This has a still further embarrassing epistemological consequence for the causal account. Recollect that what is supposed to be the cause of our experience *of* this or that, is precisely that of which, on the basis of the experience, we would claim knowledge. For example, to say in the presence of a chair, 'That's a chair' is, on the causal theory, not only to lay claim to an experience which justifies the claim made but also is to imply that it is the chair which is the cause of the validating experience. However, if the experience is the effect and the chair the cause, then, in accordance with what was said a moment ago, the chair and what I experience when I experience the chair cannot be the same.

The usual way of coping with this radical difficulty in the causal theory by those who wish to uphold it, is to build into the theory some distinction between objects as they are in themselves and objects as they appear to us. A further interpretation put upon this distinction is that what *directly* appears to us in experience as the result of stimulation of the sense-organ is a *representation* of the object which (or light or sound from which) stimulated the sense-organ and caused the experience. In explaining seeing an object as really seeing a representation of that object, the defender of the causal theory may draw upon a number of analogies which lie ready to hand. One is the relationship between a painted or photographic portrait and the sitter; the portrait appears to guarantee the existence of the sitter and, moreover, puts us in possession of information about some of his characteristics. It is worth recollecting, however, that some portraits can be so bad as to make it quite impossible to recognise the originals from them. So the question is bound to arise: how do we know whether the images or representations which sense-experience affords are true to their originals or not? Clearly, answering this is going to require some comparison with the originals, but we can never do this. If all that appears is the representation, we are never in a position to check what it is a representation of.

Furthermore there is a difficulty about how some experiences could be representations. Representations are primarily visual and only secondarily and by analogy, non-visual. But how can one consider a smell, a taste or even a sound as a representation of anything? The most usual way out of this difficulty, found in classic form in Locke, is to mark off those qualities of experiences which could be (and in Locke's view are) exact representations of the causing object and those which could not be.

The former qualities, following Locke's terminology, are commonly called primary and the latter secondary. Primary qualities, e.g. shape and other spatial properties, thus characterise both the representation and the object, while secondary qualities, e.g. colour, loudness and pitch of sounds, warmth, taste, smell, etc. characterise the representation only, and are caused by something different in kind—in fact certain primary qualities of the object. For example the pitch of the sound of a bell depends on the shape of the bell and the speed of motion of the bell clapper; similarly experienced red depends ultimately on the fact that the surface texture of the object reflects or transmits light of certain frequencies and absorbs light of others. Consequently *in themselves* objects possess only primary qualities and no secondary ones, i.e. they are not in themselves coloured, smelly, loud, shrill, etc.

This is hardly the position of common-sense, yet it seems a consequence of the scientific causal account of perception which is so widely accepted as to seem commonsensical. On the other hand it raises even more acutely the general difficulty of the causal view—how if we experience only representations can we know that in some qualities they resemble the objects causing them and in some not? If we try close scientific observation of the object we only get more representations. This illustrates the general point that epistemological analysis and argument often reveals paradoxes and inconsistencies in what is widely accepted.

While some philosophers, and especially physiologically-minded philosophers, still defend the causal theory in some form, many philosophers have attempted to analyse perception without invoking the causal account as its basis. To do this is to put forward a purer form of the empiricist emphasis on the primacy of experience than is to be found in Locke and other upholders of the causal theory. For we have seen that the causal form of empiricist accounts leaves us with a cause of experience which is not itself experienced but merely *inferred*. This is certainly inconsistent with a radical empiricism which employs the working hypothesis that all existence is experienced existence. Indeed, it was the detection of *transcendental,* i.e. in principle non-empirical, elements in Locke's philosophy that set his great successors Berkeley and Hume in search of a more radical empiricism. Crudely and briefly, they set out to reconstruct our knowledge of the world purely on the basis of direct experience itself without any reference to objects as they are in themselves and independently of experience. They did not begin with the assumption that the relationship in which a perceiver stands to his world is one which, as in the causal theory, presupposes the existence of that world. Rather, they took as their initial starting-point what we can term the certainty of sense-experience. In this choice is reflected the epistemological concern with indubitability which is characteristic of perceptual theorising. The examples noted at the outset of this discussion ('The water boiled at 100°C' and so on) were called observation statements and we suggested that they are grounded in particular seeings, smellings, touchings, hearings and tastings. If it can be shown that these last are indubitable as to their existence and nature, and if we can also trace a path from them to the subject-matter of an observation statement, then we shall have demonstrated the certainty of observation statements.

On the face of it, it does seem as if statements reporting particular acts of sense are indubitable. Usually two grounds for holding this are given. The first is that whenever we experience something we know that we are experiencing it. We might put this by saying that we are necessarily conscious of our sense-experiences or, alternatively, that sense-experience is self-transparent. Certainly, there does seem something odd, if not self-contradictory, in the idea of seeing, feelings, smelling or tasting something but not being aware that one is doing so. However, we should remember that the certainty *that* one is seeing or hearing does not imply certainty about *what* one is seeing or hearing. One may see vague outlines and hear chords of whose resolution one is ignorant.

The second ground for holding to the indubitability of the

deliverances of our senses is more complicated. It consists in the application of a method of systematic doubt to a straightforward perceptual situation, for example, looking at a tomato (the example is due to H. H. Price, whose work in this field has the commendable virtues of clarity and simplicity). It seems that whatever doubts we might conceivably entertain about what we were seeing, even to the extent of supposing that the tomato was really on a par with the alcoholic's pink elephant, we could not deny that we were seeing something red and of a round, bulgy shape. What the application of this systematic doubt leaves us with—in this example the red, round, bulgy 'something'—has generally been called in recent years a *sense-datum*. It is akin to what Locke called, misleadingly, an *idea*, and Hume, less misleadingly, an *impression*. One further point about sense-data should be stressed: the strong tendency to think of them as little visual images should be resisted. It is the intention of the philosophers who deal in sense-data as the foundation stones of knowledge to accord to each sense its appropriate data. Thus, if I am listening to the National Anthem with my eyes closed, what is indubitable about this experience is the series of aural sense-data (experienced sounds) into which the whole experience decomposes. These are certainly not images. Nevertheless, there is a persistent tendency to interpret sense-data as primarily visual and there are a number of reasons for this. One is that vision is practically speaking a most useful sense. It appears to discern shape and size of objects, at a distance as well as close to. Another reason derives from a common context of epistemological discussion, namely, that of proving the existence of the external world which is a spatial world of distributed bodies. Vision seems to afford us our primary perception of spatiality.

On the face of it the existence of sense-data seems almost a matter of common sense. But problems arise as soon as we turn to the task of reconstructing our common-sense notions of the perceived world in terms of them. What, for instance, is the relationship between the series of visual sense-data that are afforded me by walking round a tomato and the tomato itself? Remember that we have ruled out the causal theory's answer that the tomato is, in itself, the cause of sense-data.

One answer that might be given is that they are *appearings* of the tomato. This, while intelligible, only leads on to the odd question of how the tomato is related to its manifold appearings. Another answer that might be given is that the visual sense-data are parts of the surface of the tomato, a kind of epistemological skin. One objection to this is that each datum in this case consists not only of an appearance of the tomato but also of the background against which it appears. A more important objection is that the data often conflict with each other or with what we take to be the properties of the object's surface: for example, when a dish looks round from one viewpoint and elliptical from another, can the round and the elliptical datum *both* be parts of the dish's surface? Though this sort of conflict is less in evidence in the case of the tomato, it does render implausible the generalised thesis that sense-data are parts of object surfaces.

A further gambit of a radical kind in relating objects to their appearances is to dispose altogether with the assumption that sense-data in any way exist and to regard talk about sense-data as talk about the kind of evidence we have or could have for the existence of a material object. This view is known as *phenomenalism*. It contains a strong element of paradox when one comes to consider the existence of any object when no one is perceiving it. Traditional sense-datum theorists took the bull by the horns here and postulated the existence of unsensed sense-data. (To overcome the apparent contradiction in this, some of them called sense-data *sensibilia*, and talked of sense and unsensed *sensibilia*.) Phenomenalists cannot take this line. What they do instead is to suggest that references to unsensed objects, for example, the joists beneath the floor of this room, are references to appearances of those objects *if* they were appearing to someone. How what we regard as an actual though unperceived object can be also regarded as a set of possibilities is not explained by these theorists: those who draw cheques on merely possible credit accounts do not end up as rich men. One thing brought out by this brand of phenomenalism is that debates about the existence and nature of objects in the external world are conducted in terms of actual and possible seeings, hearings, touchings, smellings and so on. But phenomenalism in any form seems too desperate a remedy for the gulf fixed between the ordinary uncritical belief in enduring material objects and the evanescent, sporadic appearances of them in people's experience.

By now we have touched upon what will seem a large and confusing number of theories about perceptual knowledge, none of which appears to be wholly satisfactory. Once more the uncritical certitudes of common sense dissolve under the persistent questioning of the epistemologist. The search for an indubitable foundation of knowledge in sense-experience seems as foredoomed and abortive as the attempt, in the philosophy of induction, to close the gap between 'some' and 'all'. It is this pessimism that has provided one of the chief planks in the rationalist platform. Failure to locate certainties in experience leads the rationalist to seek elsewhere. In particular, he looks to reason, unaided by sense, to provide basic certainties in terms of which our knowledge can be reconstructed. I shall briefly describe and discuss two connected aspects of the rationalist position, first, the way in which mathematics operates as a rationalist ideal of knowledge and secondly, the way in which rationalism tends to involve the idea of self-evident necessary truths.

Mathematics appears to afford examples of absolutely certain and incontestable truths that are known independently of experience. The philosophical technical terms for such truths is *a priori*, which is simply a Latin phrase meaning 'from before', in this case from before experience, in contrast to things which can only be known *a posteriori*, that is after some experience. Examples of *a priori* truths in mathematics would be the simple geometrical theorem that the angles at the base of an isoceles triangle are equal or the simple arithmetical truth that $2+2=4$. The reason why one wants to say that these are *a priori* is that no conceivable experience seems relevant to *establishing* their truth or their falsity, even though experiences may be helpful in getting people to see their truth. It seems quite impossible to think of any way in which the world might change and, as a consequence, render them false. In this they contrast sharply with an empirical generalisation such as, 'All swans are white'. We can easily conceive of and describe circumstances in which this would be false (indeed, we know it is false), namely a world in which black swans have been observed. Furthermore, it is not just the generality of this example which provides the contrast, for, as we have seen in dealing with the empiricist's treatment of perception, there is room for doubt over the truth of a report such as, 'Fido is barking'. I might be both hearing and seeing things. But our two mathematical examples don't seem open to any such doubts or conceivable refutation as these two last examples. So it seems that we have at last found examples of absolutely certain statements. It is at this point that the idea of self-evidence can be brought in to back up the claim that reason alone can afford important knowledge. For it might be argued that the examples of *a priori* truths considered so far form in subject-matter a very restricted class. So the rationalistic philosopher is committed to finding more important and interesting examples than these. Epistemologically, they will be of the same kind, namely *a priori* and self-evidently necessary, such that there falsity is inconceivable. Also, once in possession of some interesting truths of this kind, the rationalist philosopher hopes to follow the example of mathematics in deriving deductively further truths from them, just as in Euclidean geometry we derive a large number of theorems from the basic axioms, postulates and definitions. Now just as we are familiar in modern mathematics with the idea of a plurality of different but self-consistent geometrical systems, so in the history of philosophy we find a number of different but putatively self-consistent rationalist systems. The purest examples are those of the great seventeenth- and eighteenth-century rationalists Descartes, Spinoza and Leibniz. Indeed the *Ethics* of Spinoza is explicitly developed in geometrical style with a full apparatus of axioms, definitions, theorems and corollaries. This is not the place to develop a detailed critique of the starting-points chosen by these great rationalist philosophers, but we can make about rationalism and the rationalistic enterprise a general critical point which is widely accepted today by philosophers. It can be developed by returning once more to the rationalist paradigm of mathematics.

While one may give unstinting recognition to the certitude of mathematics, one must realise that a price is paid for this certitude. The reason why mathematical propositions are secure from refutation at the hands of experience is precisely that they are not in any sense about experience or what is found in experience. (See also Plato's views on geometry, p. 61.) Once this is grasped, then the claim that no conceivable experience could refute $2+2=4$ appears as nothing to write home about to the epistemologist. The case has been cooked from the start in the sense that what the statement $2+2=4$ is about—if, indeed, it is about anything at all—is not some thing or things to be found in experience. Naïvely, we might say it is about numbers and we might also be inclined to suppose that in our experience of twins and string quartets we experience numbers. But this clearly won't do; in listening to four string players I do not in any way listen to, feel, see, etc. the number four. So even if $2+2=4$ is held to be about numbers, it hardly seems possible to argue that numbers are experienced by anyone. If this is correct, then it is hardly surprising that $2+2=4$ is immune from empirical refutation (or confirmation, for that matter).

Nor should the fact that mathematics can be applied to experience mislead us into thinking that it is about experience. The statement, 'One rabbit plus one rabbit equals two rabbits' is not the same statement as '$1+1=2$'. That the former is clearly about empirical matters, namely rabbits, does not entail that the latter is. It is true that we can employ mathematical techniques in the formulation of laws of nature. Consider, for example, Ohm's law for an electrical circuit, $\frac{E}{I}=R$, where $E=$voltage, $I=$current and $R=$the electrical resistance of the circuit. This, as it stands, is in algebraic form, and it becomes a statement of applied arithmetic when we assign specific numerical values to E, I and R. But consider what is involved in this. We have to find ways of measuring voltage, current and resistance so that these can be expressed in numerical terms. In any given case of measuring these quantities there is no necessity about the answer we shall get. Where, if at all, the necessity does come in, is over computing the third value, given two of the others. If we rely solely on such a computation for assigning the third value, then we are clearly *supposing* the truth of Ohm's law in so doing. If called upon to validate the law, we should not be able to rely exclusively on the mathematics involved. We should have to check the results of computation against actual observations and measurements of the phenomena. What, however, we can say is that mathematics does provide us with a potent instrument for expressing formal relationships between physical quantities. But this does not imply that these relationships, as expressed in laws, have the same status as the necessary truths of mathematics.

What this points to is the difficulty that one has in establishing matters of fact by *a priori* means, that is independently of experience. Or, to put it in a way that amounts to the same thing, it is difficult to find any statement about a matter of fact which is necessarily true and established by *a priori* means. This formulation gives us yet a further way of characterising the rationalist enterprise: a rationalist seeks to establish indubitable factual conclusions on the basis of reason alone. Putting it in this way brings out the basic contrast with empiricism, which assumes that it is only by paying attention to sense-experience that we come to learn facts. Just as the price the empiricist would appear to pay in his enterprise is the relinquishing of certainty, so there is a case for saying that the rationalist buys indubitability only at the price of ceasing to speak about experience. The history of philosophy confirms this contrast: philosophers of a rationalist cast of mind from Plato to the present all tend to dismiss common experience as a realm of mere appearance hiding, unless we step beyond it, true realities. In this tendency one finds exhibited the close connexion between the apparently ingenious trivialities of epistemological discussion and the grand, if monumental, constructions of rationalist philosophy. The poet T. S. Eliot once remarked that metaphysical systems go up like rockets and come down like sticks. To develop the metaphor in terms of our discussion, one might say that what powers the rocket and produces its display is the desire to establish large and certain conclusions, but that when this constructive and imaginative desire has burnt itself out, what falls to earth is only some radical misconception concerning, for example, what mathematical statements are about.

3
Metaphysics

W. H. Walsh

A beginner in metaphysics can be given only the roughest idea of the subject-matter and scope of this branch of enquiry. Philosophers in the past have described metaphysics as the study of 'what there is', or again have said that it is concerned to 'give an account of reality as a whole'. The first description is confusing, for it is obvious when we think about it that the physical sciences too investigate 'what there is' when they enquire into the fundamental constitution of the material universe: is metaphysics supposed to be their rival? Some idea of the difference between the two comes out when we observe that metaphysicians do not so much challenge scientific accounts of the material world as wonder if everything that exists is material; they are concerned with such questions as whether mind and matter are ultimately different kinds of thing, whether the first may not be seen as only a by-product or manifestation of the second. Does there exist, whether in the world we know in everyday experience or beyond it, a being whose nature is not material at all, for example the purely spiritual being which constitutes the God of theology? However we seek to deal with these questions, it seems plain that they do not arise in any departmental enquiry, where physics and mathematics and history are taken as examples of such enquiries. They belong to a more general study, which professes to give an account of reality as a whole. But this description too can be misleading. We all know how, in these days of increasing specialisation, arrangements for co-ordinating different investigators' results are more and more necessary; without such arrangements knowledge may advance in particular fields, but the general shape of the advance cannot become clear. It is important in our present circumstances that there should be persons ready to play the part of intellectual contact men, but it is a mistake to think that philosophers can fill this role, except incidentally. For though philosophers, and metaphysical philosophers in particular, claim to take a synoptic as opposed to a piecemeal view of the world, they do it not by co-ordinating empirical results but by comparing whole outlooks or intellectual schemes. They ask, for example, what we are to make of man in the light of what is established about him by psychologists and physiologists on the one hand, and what is taken for granted on the other in his daily dealings with his fellow men, in literature or in courts of law. Are men genuine agents, answerable for what they do, or are they mere automata, responding mechanically to external stimuli? In facing such questions the metaphysician will clearly need to know what is going on in a diversity of fields. But he will be less interested in details than in general ways of thinking, and he will not allow preoccupation with new ideas to blind him to the existence of older ones which continue to function in important areas of life. His aim will be to assess rather than merely co-ordinate advances, in order to arrive, if possible, at a balanced picture which does not ignore the latest scientific claims but equally does not swallow them quite uncritically.

In this essay I shall attempt to introduce metaphysics by considering two problems in particular which have preoccupied Western philosophers almost throughout philosophical history: mind and body, and the existence of God. The somewhat abstract points adumbrated above will become clearer to the reader if he first enters into the details of the problems that follow, and then reflects on the issues bearing in mind these introductory remarks.

Mind and Body

Is a human being a unitary something, possessing different aspects which we categorise as mental and physical but which cannot exist in separation? Or should he be thought of, in the terms used by some earlier philosophers, as 'a spirit inhabiting a body'? A combination of factors, philosophical and extra-philosophical, have inclined a large number of philosophers to accept the second answer. They were in the first place aware of the contrast drawn in religious discourse between soul and body, a contrast which is most readily interpreted as implying that man not only has a dual nature, but is, in a way which remains to be explained, a being compounded of two wholly different things, one spiritual, the other material. The human body, like all other bodies, is subject to decay and disintegration; the human soul, it was argued, is a different kind of thing altogether and hence can survive bodily death. At an early stage of thought the soul was thought of as being material in substance: the Latin word 'anima' means 'wind' and 'breath' as well as 'soul'. But Socrates (470–399 B.C.) in Plato's (427–347 B.C.) dialogue *Phaedo* already had the idea of the soul as something immaterial, whose nature it was to be simple and which hence differed utterly from the body in which it was, in his view, temporarily imprisoned. (The date of the *Phaedo* and the accuracy with which Plato reports Socrates' views are matters of controversy.) And though its Jewish origins precluded Christianity from embracing this opinion entirely (it is to the resurrection of the body that Christians look forward at the Last Judgement), the idea was all the same continuously influential with philosophers both in the Middle Ages, when philosophy was largely the handmaid of theology, and in the more secular environment of the seventeenth and eighteenth centuries. It is instructive in this connexion to observe how, towards the end of this period, Immanuel Kant, a major critic of the pretensions of metaphysics, rejected a formal dualism of mind and body only to set up in its place a not dissimilar dualism of flesh and spirit. The same philosopher, again, though hostile to organised religion in the customary eighteenth-century manner, nevertheless included the immortality of the soul as one of his two articles of 'moral belief'. As was the case with others at the time, his repudiation of the externals of Christianity concealed from him the extent to which the central tenets of Christian doctrine still commanded his allegiance.

It would, all the same, be absurd to suggest that philosophical commitment to mind/body dualism rests only on its fitting in with commonly accepted religious views. There were many arguments for the doctrine at the purely philosophical level, and some of these we must now explore.

Let me begin by mentioning a set of considerations which were influential both in antiquity and again in the seventeenth century, when René Descartes produced his classical statement of the case for believing that mind and body were, as he put it, 'really distinct', though intimately combined and 'commingled' in this life. One of the earliest preoccupations of Western philosophers was with questions about knowledge. What conditions have to be fulfilled, they asked, if we are to be said to have knowledge as opposed to mere belief, and in what circumstances can we hope to fulfil these conditions. A natural answer to the first of these questions is that we can be said to have knowledge when we have adequate grounds for the claims we put forward, and that our grounds are adequate when what we claim to know is within the range of our senses. And this carries with it an answer to the second question: we can hope to attain knowledge if our sense-organs are in good order and if the conditions of their operation are at least as good as normal (if the light is satisfactory when it is a matter of using the eyes, and so on). Answers on these lines have been put forward by philosophers of an *empiricist* turn of mind from an early date; but equally there have never been lacking critics of such answers. (Empiricism and some of the main difficulties in it are discussed more fully in Chapter 2, pp. 42 ff.) One criticism particularly relevant to our present enquiry was advanced by Plato in his dialogue, the *Theaetetus*, where he argued that even if it was a necessary condition of obtaining knowledge that our sense-organs should be functioning properly, it was not in itself enough to ensure that knowledge was obtained. For as well as noting that, for example, the thing now before my eyes is bright or shiny or larger than some other object, I need for a developed system of knowledge to be able to say such things as that it is *different* from that other object, though *identical* with it in colour; that each of them is *one*, though together they make *two*; that they are *like* in certain respects, *unlike* in others; that each of them *exists*. Which of the sense-organs is involved in judgements of this sort? Plato thought it obvious that none of the senses was here concerned, and that it was with the soul that we apprehend these important characters. The truth was that the soul both uses the senses as its instruments in the search for knowledge and also functions as an independent source of knowledge. And both these suggest that the soul is something distinct from the body.

This conclusion is reinforced for Plato by another line of argument. When we ask ourselves what kinds of truth seem to be most certain, we are apt to come up with examples of mathematical as well as simple sense knowledge. It was, in fact, particularly natural for Plato himself to think on these lines, for mathematics alone among the sciences had made anything like substantial progress in his day. Now the question can be asked: of what is the geometer thinking when he demonstrates, for example, the properties of the triangle? It cannot be said in the first place that he is thinking of the figure he draws on the blackboard or (in Plato's day) on the sand, since this will be at best an imperfect example of a triangle, having, for instance, sides which are only approximately straight. Nor can it be true that he is thinking about any other triangles he may have met with in the world, for apart from the fact that he speaks of the properties of triangles *as such*, any instance he may have met with in experience may turn out to be defective in the same way as the triangle drawn in solving the problem. Plato drew from these considerations the conclusion that geometry is not about things which are accessible to the senses at all, but is concerned with objects of quite a different kind, objects which he called 'Forms' or 'Ideas' and which he spoke of as 'intelligible' as opposed to 'sensible': open to the intelligence and not to the senses. To achieve mathematical knowledge (and the same goes, Plato believed, for scientific knowledge of any kind) a man needs a soul as well as a body, and there is every reason to think the two entirely distinct. The intellect does not depend upon the body as the senses do, and is nevertheless concerned in the acquisition of knowledge of the surest and most important kind.

Stated in this summary fashion these arguments may well seem crude and unconvincing, quite inadequate as a basis for Plato's conclusion that a man should 'pursue the truth by applying his pure and unadulterated thought to the pure and unadulterated object, cutting himself off as much as possible from his eyes and ears and virtually all the rest of his body, as an impediment which by its presence prevents the soul from attaining to truth and clear thinking' (*Phaedo*, 65–6). It is interesting, despite this, to observe that a case of a very similar kind was developed by Descartes when he took up the problem some two thousand years after Plato. Like Plato, Descartes began by attacking the claim of the senses to be the source of knowledge. We think that the everyday things around us, the objects with which we come in contact through the senses, are more surely and evidently known than anything else could be. But philosophical reflection shows this to be false: there is no item of so-called sense-knowledge which might not in principle be false, since we cannot exclude the possibility that in any particular case our senses are deceiving us. That we sometimes fail to perceive properly is evident; and if once, then why not on any subsequent occasion, since there is nothing which marks off authentic from illusory perception? Descartes follows Plato again in contrasting what he calls 'the fluctuating testimony of the senses' with clear and distinct intellectual perception; like his great predecessor he turns to mathematics for examples of genuine knowledge. But he gives a new twist to the argument by suggesting that doubt can infect not just the operations of the senses, but those of the intellect too: an evil demon might bedevil my thinking as much as my sensing. Hence the need for an ultimate answer to scepticism, which is found when a man proposes to himself the possibility that he might not exist, and sees at once that the supposition itself rules the possibility out. This argument of Descartes is summed up in a famous saying, 'Cogito, ergo sum'—'I think, therefore I am'. Even if I am deceived, I must exist to be deceived. But when I ask myself what I am whose existence is thus revealed as certain, the answer, Descartes assures us, is something whose whole nature consists in thought. I can suppose that I have no body, since my body is known to me through my senses and my senses are one and all uncertain sources of knowledge. But I cannot believe that I who entertain the possibility that I do not exist do not really exist: my existence as a thinker at least is secure. Hence my thinking self is distinct in principle from my bodily self, and is 'more easily known' than the latter.

There are many points at which this argument is open to question, but I shall not stop to discuss them here. Instead, I want to turn to a different kind of argument which Descartes uses to establish his conclusion, one whose immediate plausibility is perhaps greater than those so far considered. We customarily distinguish between material things, constituents of the physical universe, and conscious beings like ourselves which possess a mental life. At least one property which is essential to being a material thing is that it should occupy or be spread out in space: it always makes sense to ask of such an entity where it is, how large it is, and so on. Questions of this sort seem, however, to have no application to minds or their constituents: you cannot meaningfully pursue the question where my mind is located in space, or enquire into the distance between one thought and another. From these facts Descartes drew the conclusion that the mental and material orders were entirely separate from one another; mind and matter, as he put it, were different 'substances', and every substance was, in effect, self-contained. Physical events represented what might be called the vicissitudes of material substance, which was continually changing its configurations but remained for all that constant in quantity: if we asked to what life-history a chemical reaction, for example, belonged, the ultimate answer must always be that of material substance as such. Similarly with mental events and processes, which were happenings in or to a mind. The mental order was different from the material, in so far as it existed in the form of separate 'thinking things' rather than as a single undifferentiated substance. But just as it was evident that there could be no physical transactions without a material substance, so there could be no mental transactions—no thoughts or experiences, feelings, perceptions or acts of will—unless there were minds in which or through which they could take place, and which would be their ultimate subject.

The Cartesian (the name 'Descartes' was originally 'des Cartes' and so 'Cartesian' is the adjective for 'of Descartes') doctrine of substance has often been criticised as an indefensible survival from mediaeval thought, but it is important to notice that Descartes' case here does not collapse if it is abandoned. A fundamental distinction between the material and mental orders is maintained by many philosophers whose outlook is in other respects very different from Descartes'. And it is not surprising that this should be so, for thoughts and experiences certainly seem on the face of it to be very different things from movements of matter. The latter take place unthinkingly, the former are conscious almost by definition. Hence any attempt to reduce the mental to the material, to make out, as Behaviourists have done, for example, that thoughts are *simply* movements in the larynx, seems doomed to failure from the start. Even if it is true, as it often appears to be, that our experiences have physical conditions, it will not be true that they are in any real sense physical occurrences. Conversely physical occurrences, whatever their nature, cannot be identified with thoughts, which means that the 'thinking' attributed to computers, however remarkable, is not thinking in the strict sense. Computers are not conscious and therefore *cannot* think.

I shall return to these issues presently, but meantime must again mention that if Descartes advanced powerful reasons for the distinction of mind and body, he did not believe them to be in fact distinct in this life. My mind and my body, he said, 'compose a certain unity'; I am not lodged in my body as a pilot is lodged in a ship, but am 'intimately conjoined' with it. Unfortunately the details of this doctrine remain exceedingly obscure, both in Descartes and in the theories of his successors. A central difficulty can be brought out if we ask how mind and body are supposed to be related when they compose a unity: are they, as is normally claimed, in causal interaction? Common sense certainly suggests that mental happenings can have bodily effects and vice versa, but the Cartesian doctrine of substance as self-contained strictly precluded the acceptance of what was called *transeunt* causation (causation between things of a different order, as opposed to within one order), and some followers of Descartes were driven to say, most implausibly, that mind/body interaction is apparently only, the truth being that God causes changes to take place in the body *on the occasion of* mental changes which happen quite independently, and similarly causes changes in the mind of the occasion of bodily changes. Now though this difficulty about the kind of causation required for mind/body interaction diminished when the doctrine of substance was discredited, it can hardly be said to have disappeared altogether. Physiologists who give an account of the physical process of perception, for instance, still feel uneasy about the fact that the process leads up to a certain state of activity in the brain and then terminates in a conscious experience, something of a different order altogether. How, they ask, does such an experience relate to a brain state, and how can it be consequent on a change which is, after all, physical? This difficulty has indeed led to a modern denial of both mind/body interaction and dualism, namely the identity hypothesis which is discussed below (p. 74).

The foregoing discussion may suggest that, when mind and body enter on their union, they do so as independent things and somehow retain their independence throughout. That Descartes himself took a view of this general sort seems certain, but all the same he did not subscribe to it in a crude form. There were, he argued, three types of activity in which human beings engage. Some, such as walking, they performed as possessed of a body; others, such as seeing the connexion between the premisses of an argument and its conclusion, in their capacity as possessors of minds. But there were yet other activities which could be explained in terms neither of mind nor of body alone, but only of the whole mind/body complex: the activity of perceiving, for example. Perception from one point of view is an experience and therefore belongs to the mental order. But we can have perceptual experiences, normally at least, only when our sense-organs are operative, which means that sensing presupposes a body. Similarly with feelings and sensations. To maintain his position about knowledge Descartes argues interestingly that the senses were given us for practical purposes, to ensure the general welfare of the mind/body composite, rather than as sources of information in the strict sense. But we need not attend to this aspect of his theory now.

What we must ask instead is whether this limited concession to common sense goes anything like far enough. Descartes makes no pronouncement about the range of activities which belong to the mind/body complex, but it is clear enough that he reserves some for what we might call the pure mind and the pure body respectively. If his picture of the situation is not quite that of two independent entities entering on a union, he nevertheless thinks of them rather as two marriage partners, who bring their separate characters with them, are changed profoundly as a result of their union, but can nevertheless emerge from it as separate beings. But if mind and body really compose a unity, can they have any separate existence at all? Will *any* activities belong strictly to the one or the other? May it not be, for instance, that I show my character when I walk, if, for example, I am neurotic or self-conscious or proud? And is it quite certain that my thoughts are independent of my ability to hear and produce sounds? If I could not talk, could I think? And if the reply is that people who are dumb can certainly think, could men generally think if mankind lacked the power of speech?

It is arguable (and has indeed been argued by a number of recent philosophers) that the whole attempt to sort out human activities into watertight classes, mental, physical and mental-cum-physical, is a mistake. Either we find ourselves hesitating about the compartment into which to put particular instances (if I walk up and down or pull faces as I try to solve a philosophical difficulty, does that mean my activity is not really mental?), or we ensure against objections by putting everything in the third bracket. Nor is the difficulty confined to the classification of activities: parallel problems arise when we turn our attention to states. If I suffer from toothache am I in a mental or a physical state? Despite the fact that we commonly distinguish between physical and mental pains, and classify the pain of toothache among the former, many philosophers insist that, since pain is an experience, it can only occur in a mind and must accordingly be in all instances mental. They would agree that the pain in question is normally occasioned by physical circumstances such as decay in the tooth or exposure of the nerve, but refuse to allow that there is more to it than that. We might ask them by way of comment whether the very concept of this sort of pain does not merely presuppose a physical setting but also involve a physical condition: a pain of this sort is felt *in one's body*—it is not a happening in a spirit loosely attached to one's body. We may ask further, here following Wittgenstein, the most penetrating of recent writers on this subject, whether sense can be made of the idea of a pain which has no natural, external expression, whether of a primitive or a sophisticated variety. Of course people can and do feel pains which they contrive to keep to themselves; it is a social accomplishment, in our sort of society at least, not to manifest pain too obviously. But would physical pain be what it is if our feelings under this head had no natural expression of any kind; if it was just a matter of chance that men cry out when they are hurt, the cry having a purely incidental connexion with the pain? Yet if we once agree that having a toothache and, say, drawing breath may be two aspects of a single situation we are once more landed with something which is mental and physical at once.

The reader will appreciate that only the barest sketch of an argument has been given in this discussion; to point out the most obvious inadequacy, I have said nothing about the notion of mental pain. Even as it stands, however, the case is perhaps strong enough to suggest that we need to rethink the assumptions with which Descartes persisted even when he admitted that mind and body, in this life, 'compose a certain unity', assumptions which have been widely accepted both by supporters and opponents of the Cartesian philosophy as a whole. The most important of these is perhaps that the terms 'experience' and 'mental activity' carry with them no reference to anything physical; they could be and would properly be applied to pure, i.e. unembodied, spirits. I have tried to show that this is not so: that experiences and human activities, mental and physical alike, are to be attributed to persons, a person being something which is neither exclusively mental nor exclusively physical, nor for that matter a strange amalgam of the mental and the physical 'conjoined'. Admittedly there are many problems involved in analysing the concept of a person, but their existence does not destroy the case set out above.

Let us approach these problems by outlining an alternative to the view about mind and body which we have been examining, an alternative sketched many years ago by Aristotle and worked out at length on our own day in Gilbert Ryle's book *The Concept of Mind*. According to Plato, a man is a soul imprisoned in a body; according to Descartes, he is a mind mysteriously united with a body. On both these views mind and body are thought of as distinct things, even though they do not exist in separation. But on the Aristotelian alternative a man's mind or soul at least is not substantial at all; it is merely an aspect of his person which we find it convenient for certain purposes to abstract and treat as if it were an independent thing. When we speak of a man's mind we speak of such things as his character, personality and abilities, and these are shown in what he does and how he does it. A man with a quick and supple mind is a man who solves problems quickly and can turn his attention from one subject to another without difficulty; a lazy or idle or slow-witted person is one who, in certain sorts of situation, will tend to react in certain characteristic ways or (in the last case) will be capable only of a delayed or inappropriate reaction. It makes perfectly good sense on this view to speak of someone as having, say, a sharp mind, but as this merely means that he sees subtle distinctions or quickly grasps the point, we must not interpret it as parallel in all respects to saying that he has sharp eyes. A man with sharp eyes has a sense-organ which is in excellent condition; there is nothing similar we can point to in the case of a man with a sharp mind.. Hence the absurdity of asking for the seat of the soul and of describing it, as some of the older philosophers did, as 'the place of thoughts'. The soul is not anywhere, for the simple reason that it is not a thing of any sort.

It may be asked just how close is the tie-up between mind and body on this account. At first it seems to be very close indeed, for the most obvious way in which we manifest our abilities or dispositions is in our physical doings. One extremely important respect in which this analysis differs from that with which we were previously concerned is in the priority it gives to what Ryle calls 'knowing how' over 'knowing that'. Plato and Descartes speak as if knowing were always, or at least primarily, a matter of contemplating truths, an activity which calls for the exercise of a special part of ourselves, the intellect. Against this, Ryle argues that truths need to be used, not merely contemplated: even in the field of the pure intellect what we want is skill, the skill to build theories, for example, or to draw conclusions from premisses. But as these examples show, not all our knowledge is shown in overt activities; a man can show that he is master of elementary arithmetic by giving someone the right change, but equally he can do it by simply working out a sum in his head. To recognise this is not, however, to deny that skills, and hence knowledge, are *typically* manifested in bodily movements; if they are also shown in activities which are purely, or largely, 'mental', that is the result of subsequent refinement. As Ryle points out, it was at a comparatively late stage of human history that men acquired the ability to read to themselves; previously they could show they knew how to read only by reading out loud.

There are, however, more serious objections to the Rylean view. One which will occur to many readers concerns its account of consciousness. Descartes, as we saw, made consciousness the defining property of mind, and in doing so seemed only to follow the lead of common sense, for are we not conscious of ourselves at least throughout our waking lives? How can a view which, to put it crudely, reduces mind to character and capacities account for consciousness? This question is the more urgent because it might well be thought that it is the presence of consciousness in human beings which distinguishes them from machines. If we ask ourselves why we should not allow that a computer has a mental life, in view of the fact that it can undertake calculations beyond the capacity of a mere human being and may well develop quirks (a character) of its own, the common answer would be that there is nothing to show that a machine is conscious or has any sense of its own identity. Yet it is not apparent how this answer could be given if Ryle were correct.

Ryle tries to meet these difficulties in two ways. In the first place he argues that what he calls 'the bogy of mechanism' presents no real threat, since there are all sorts of obvious differences between men and machines. The operations performed by the most ingeniously designed machine are, however complicated, of a routine nature: they follow patterns prescribed in advance by the persons who wrote the programme. Human thought, by contrast, is or at least can be full of novelty and imagination. A machine can add up better than a human being; what evidence is there that it can write a poem or a piece of music? And there is another difference which is shown in our attitudes to, and ways of speaking about, men and machines respectively. Men, we suppose, are to some degree at least capable of initiating and controlling their own movements; they have the capacity to be independent agents. But machines do what they do only because they are caused to do it; the origin of their actions lies outside themselves. Hence the propriety of praising or blaming people for what they do, or again of expressing resentment or indignation about it: these attitudes are apposite because of the underlying assumption that the subjects concerned can alter or inhibit their behaviour if they choose to do so, and that they will make the choice if appropriate pressure is brought to bear. To praise or blame or get indignant with a machine, however, is a wholly pointless proceeding: a machine cannot help what it does, and neither encouragement nor disapproval will affect its future actions.

In assessing the performance of a machine we can have regard only to external results, but with human beings we can take account of effort and determination as well, giving marks for trying as well as actual achievement. Would it even make sense to think of a machine as trying or intending to some something? And if not, can a machine be said to *act* at all in the strict sense of that word?

Arguments on these lines are often met with in the writings of contemporary British and American philosophers. Whereas earlier thinkers conceived of the soul as the source of true knowledge or the seat of consciousness, the modern tendency is to describe it in terms of agency. The soul, as Plato already said, has the capacity to be self-moving, and this is what differentiates it from everything which is merely material. But though this offers a solution of a sort to the pressing contemporary problem about men and machines, it does not in itself provide answers to the questions about the simplicity or duality of human nature which Plato and Descartes raised. That this is so we can see if we ask: is it men who on this view are to be taken as agents, or are they agents only because of the activity of something separable within them? Many modern philosophers are disposed by temperament and general conviction to say it is men or persons, not separate selves, which act. But their reasons for taking this view are by no means immediately evident.

To see what is involved here we must return to the second point in Ryle's defence. To the charge that his theory leaves no room for the all-important concept of consciousness Ryle replies that this concept has been gravely misunderstood by past philosophers. Consciousness is not, as they were apt to suppose, a mysterious inner light which never goes out; it is rather a certain sort of preparedness, analysable in terms of what would be the case if various contingencies arose rather than of what is going on now. A man who drives with conscious care may be outwardly like any other driver: the difference comes in the extent to which he is ready to jam on the brakes or take avoiding action, the frequency with which he looks in his mirror and otherwise observes the general traffic situation, the frame of mind in which he carries out the whole driving operation. To do something consciously is thus to do it in a particular manner: it is not to do it and at the same time do something else, namely engage in observation of non-physical activities within oneself.

In criticism of Ryle and of others who have attempted to give this deflationary account of consciousness, it has often been said that they are deeply prejudiced against the inner life: they leave out of consideration the central fact that through consciousness we have a special sort of access to ourselves which no one else can possibly have. And it is certainly true that Ryle is never tired of denouncing the theory of 'privileged access', according to which only the owner of a mind can properly pronounce on what is going on in that mind. We in fact know a great deal about the minds of others, Ryle protests: frequently we know just what they are thinking and feeling, and sometimes we know them better than they know themselves, for example when they are of a vain or jealous character. But this could be granted without our having to admit that there are no circumstances in which a person is in a special position to report on his private mental happenings. Take for example an occasion on which I am silently turning some matter over in my mind, and you ask me what it is: might I not claim to be in a uniquely favourable position to answer this sort of question? Of course there are circumstances in which men tend to answer such questions falsely, when they are ashamed of their thoughts, for instance, but the point here is that the falsehood is deliberate: they know what was really in their mind all the time. Similarly with sensations and feelings: although, as we mentioned earlier, social considerations often lead us to give a misleading account of these when called on to declare them, it seems natural even so to say that here again the person concerned must know what is going on in him as no one else can. But if this is so, privileged access is in effect preserved, and with it an important part of the traditional account of consciousness.

Recent philosophy has contained many acute discussions of points arising in this general area, in the course of which a number of ancient assumptions have been wholly discredited. The idea that each of us starts as a private centre of consciousness, aware directly only of himself and having to establish what is going on outside him by a series of precarious inferences, is a case in point. If the life of the mind is to be described as private, its privacy must contrast with the state of something else which is not private but is all the same directly accessible: the common public world. Nor are the contents of the mind as individual and personal as philosophers like Locke supposed: the ways in which I think and react are, broadly speaking, the result of my education and, like language itself, constitute a social rather than an individual accomplishment. I am certainly not wholly isolated in a world known only to myself. But all this could be true without our being committed to a Rylean reduction of the inner life to external behaviour. Consciousness could be an important characteristic of mind even if it was agreed not to be its defining characteristic. It might be the case that we know certain things about ourselves which other people are not in a position to know directly, even though these are not the only things to know about ourselves. And most people who have no philosophical axes to grind would say that this is obviously the situation in which we live.

Why should philosophers be reluctant, or at least hesitant, about accepting this description of the situation? The answer is to be found in their search for a viable alternative to the dualism favoured by Plato and Descartes. Previously man was thought of as a spirit inhabiting a body; now we are urged to think of him as a person, the latter term being taken to cover a single entity possessed of both mental and physical characteristics. Descartes oscillated between saying that the term 'I' referred exclusively to his mind and allowing that it might, in certain circumstances, be taken to stand for the whole mind/body complex; those who take up an anti-Cartesian position insist that it always refers to what is mental and physical at once. It is the same I which is thinking these thoughts and putting them down on paper. But if the Cartesian doctrine of consciousness is preserved, even in an attenuated form, it looks as if the 'I' will be, after all, dual-centred, in so far as it will present itself in one way to the person concerned and in another to others: I shall know some things about myself directly, others will have to find out about me by studying my behaviour. What then becomes of the unity of the person? And what in any case are we to make of the apparently undeniable fact that personal experience and bodily functioning are wholly different sorts of things? No doubt I could not think unless my brain were in a certain state, but does that show that thinking *is* having certain things happening in one's brain? Yet unless we can argue for a solution on those lines talk about persons will be no more than a cover for ignorance, and no proper alternative to dualism will exist.

It is at this point that we must consider the identity hypothesis. The hypothesis, put crudely, is that when a man is said to be engaged in mental activity or to be in a mental state, a single set of events is going on which, however, presents itself under two different aspects. Under one aspect it presents itself to the person concerned as a series of experiences, while under the other aspect, i.e. for external observers or rather for scientifically-informed external observers, it is a series of happenings in the brain. The great difference in character between the two aspects of this one set of events lies in the great difference in the two modes of observation of it. The person concerned has an actor's not a spectator's view, as it were: he directly experiences or introspects the mental events, while the external observer has to rely on sense-organs and scientific instruments. A partial analogy would be perception of one object by different senses, e.g. wine appears red to sight, cool to touch, and tart to taste; it is all along the same wine but different senses reveal different characteristics of it. Similarly when a person is thinking of his holidays or feeling pain the two mental activities may appear to him as imagery or unpleasant sensations respectively, but to the external observer they appear as different types of brain activity. Activity elsewhere in the body may be involved, but, on this view, only as a consequence or cause of the brain activity, and thus not identifiable with the mental activity. Were someone to ask which of these aspects is to be preferred, the answer on one form of the theory is neither: each is appropriate to a basic mode of observation, and there can be no question of wiping out one or the other. But there is also in existence a more radical form of the identity theory which argues that that one aspect and mode of observation is superior. What from a distance we take to be a cloud turns out as we fly into it to be drops of water; we experience it from a distance as a white fleecy thing, but it on closer and more accurate observation is really quite different. Similarly, the suggestion is, what presents itself to us as immediately experienced thoughts and feelings are really nothing more than electrical changes in the brain; the immediate experience is subjective and elusive, but science shows or (as it develops, will show) the true cerebral nature of mental events. And if this suggestion were accepted we should really have an alternative to Descartes: a man would be a living body, and nothing else.

Unfortunately neither form of the identity hypothesis is quite convincing. The first is unable to eradicate the last vestiges of dualism, for the two aspects amount to two orders or modes of existence, or, worse still, they are mere appearances of an unknown underlying reality. The second eradicates dualism, but only by arbitrary fiat, for after all who is to say that experiences are really nothing but brain states? To learn about physical processes we go to the scientist, but why should we suppose that scientists have any particular qualifications to pronounce on experiences? Nor indeed is it true that physiologists and others who work in these fields are able to identify the brain states which correspond to particular thoughts and feelings, though they can point to the counterparts of more general conditions such as a state of excitement. The scientific basis on which the identity hypothesis rests is thus no more than speculative, even if it is reasonable to expect that it will become less uncertain as empirical research proceeds.

Scientific work has a bearing on the philosophical problem of mind and body, but it has no more than a bearing. Philosophers will continue to be interested in the achievements of physiologists and computer designers, and these achievements will sometimes give new twists to old philosophical problems. But they will not in themselves produce philosophical solutions, if only for the reason mentioned at the beginning of this chapter, that the philosopher's task is to look at his problems for many points of view. The results of scientific enquiry must naturally be respected by the philosopher, since they constitute part of the data about which he is trying to philosophise. It is important to stress, however, that he has other allegiances as well as to the scientist: he must take account of the data of immediate experience and common life in addition to those the scientist provides. Except on these conditions he cannot hope to provide an overall view. And just because this is his situation, he is involved in a continuing debate which is not quite like the debates of scientists or mathematicians (except so far as these are really philosophical), a debate in which conflicting positions are continuously refined but in which no single view can finally claim to have achieved a definite victory. As in the case of literature, reflection on these issues can have the effect of adding to our understanding, without increasing our knowledge of the world in any literal sense.

The Existence of God

I turn now to my second main problem, the existence of God. I shall assume that it is not necessary to offer any detailed explanation of the interest philosophers take in this question, since in this case it is plainly shared by thinking persons generally. But it is important to make certain preliminary observations before considering the arguments which have been advanced on one side or the other.

First, we must notice that when a philosopher sets out to prove or disprove the existence of God he is not usually using the term 'God' in its full religious sense. The God of the Christian religion, as spoken of in the scriptures for instance, has the qualities of a loving father and a judge who is at once just and merciful; such a God is a proper object of worship. The God philosophers discuss is sometimes described by them as 'the perfect being', but 'perfect' in this context is not a moral expression. When a philosopher says that God is the being who possesses all perfections, the attributes he has in mind are such things as omniscience and omnipotence, the power of existing outside or throughout time, the power of being free from change, as in this sentence from Descartes:

> By the name God I understand a substance that is infinite, eternal, immutable, independent, all-knowing, all-powerful, and by which I myself and everything else . . . have been created.

A believer might well comment that the existence or non-existence of a God so described was a matter of indifference to him. But if he did make this comment the proper thing to do would be to refer him to the writings of theologians, where God is spoken of in similarly abstract terms. We should not forget in this connexion that philosophical preoccupation with the existence of God itself originated in theology; it was part of an attempt to think out the theoretical basis of religion. There is, of course, much more to religion than theory, so much so that to many of those directly concerned in them religious activities hardly seem to involve any theoretical claims at all. Religion, for such people, is a matter of faith, or of works, or of having a pure heart. We may wonder, even so, whether it really *makes sense* unless certain things are true, and it is with their truth that the philosopher is concerned. The God of philosophy may not be identical with the God of religion, but if we can make nothing of the first we may well find ourselves in difficulties when we try to hang on to the second.

A second point which we must consider briefly at this preliminary stage is just what is involved in 'proving existence'. The phrase itself is far from lucid, and indeed there are few occasions when ordinary persons find themselves required to prove the existence of anything. Even in courts of law disputes about existence are rare, though the courts are quite often called upon to decide related questions about identity, to determine, for example, whether the man in the dock was the very same man who was seen to climb over the wall with a sack on his back. One sort of context in which we are faced with really proving the existence of something or (more commonly) someone, is that in which we possess a certain description and have to determine whether or not there is anything it fits. The French police at the time of the Revolution, for example, no doubt formed the idea that the escapes of aristocrats were being organised and carried through by a single person or organisation: their problem was then to decide if there really was such a person or organisation. The problem could be approached by considering the details of the various escapes and determining whether they showed clear evidence of having been planned and carried out by a master mind. And it could be said to be solved once the police acquired knowledge of the existence of the Scarlet Pimpernel and were able to satisfy themselves that he was the man behind the escapes.

In this kind of case it is plain that the question of existence turns on particular facts; it is, at bottom, an empirical matter. But not all questions about existence are of this kind. Consider, for instance, a situation in which someone enquires if there is a number between 743 and 762 which is divisible by 23. Do we decide this by looking at the facts? One difficulty in saying that we do is that it is not clear that we should properly describe the number series as existing in fact, since numbers are not space-and-time existents in the way in which trees and people are. But a more important difference from the previous example is that, while you or I may get the answer by simply trying the possibilities in turn, a mathematician can use other methods. For it will be obvious to him that whether or not such a number exists depends on the rules by which the system of natural numbers as a whole is constructed. It is not a contingent fact, which could well have been otherwise, that there is a number which answers the description given, but a matter of necessity to be demonstrated from those rules. And it follows that the enquiry in this case does not turn on empirical considerations (See also Chapter 2, pp 54 ff).

If we turn now to philosophical attempts to prove God's

existence, the first point that must strike us is that they do not answer precisely to either of the two patterns just outlined. Some of them indeed begin with the rehearsal of familiar facts, and so have the appearance of being empirical. This is the case with, for example, the celebrated Argument from Design, which calls attention to the immense amount of order and beauty in the universe and maintains that its presence can be explained only if the world was fashioned by a Great Designer. Another instance of the same thing is found in Descartes, who held that the very fact that he had the idea of God proved the existence of God: the content of the idea was such that only God could have originated it. But there are other arguments in this field which are commonly classified as empirical and which yet differ strikingly from the Scarlet Pimpernel case. The existence of the Pimpernel was finally made certain because the Pimpernel left his special mark on whatever he did; Descartes, in the argument just referred to, similarly thought that God left his mark on his handiwork, man, in the shape of the unique idea of God. But in the proof which attempts to show that God must exist as a First or Ultimate Cause—a proof which goes back to Plato, and of which versions are found in Aquinas, Leibniz and Spinoza, among others—a start is made from an exceedingly general fact: it is stated that 'something' exists (since I at least exist), or that 'the world' exists, and then argued that because the something in question, or the world, is 'finite' or limited, it must ultimately owe its existence to something else, which is infinite and unlimited. In another common version of this proof the argument runs as follows: the existence of something contingent is certain, therefore the existence of something necessary is certain, and this necessary being is God. To describe the existence of a thing as 'contingent', on this way of speaking, is to say that it depends causally on the existence of something else; by contrast a 'necessary being' is supposed to exist 'through itself alone', i.e. to be its own cause. It is obvious that none of us exists through himself alone, and therefore that there are contingent beings in the terms of the argument. But it is equally obvious that whether or not the proof succeeds turns not on the truth of this statement, which is uncontroversial, but on whether the move from contingent to necessary is legitimate. And however we describe that question, it is not a straightforward empirical issue.

So far I have been concerned with arguments which profess to ground God's existence in experience. But in addition to these causal or empirical proofs philosophers have adduced considerations of an entirely different kind in support of the thesis that God exists, considerations which depend on the content of ideas or the meaning of words rather than on the nature of things. The most celebrated of these *a priori* (*'a priori'* see p. 52) arguments is that first propounded by St. Anselm in the eleventh century and later known as the Ontological Proof. St. Anselm held that the very idea of God was such that God's existence was certain: we had only to reflect on what was meant by 'God' to see that God could not not exist. The idea of God is the idea of a being than which nothing greater can be conceived. Now if we say that such a being exists in the understanding only, it will be possible to form the idea of something greater, because existent in reality. So the being in question, that than which nothing greater can be conceived, cannot merely exist in the understanding, but must also exist in reality. Or as some later philosophers put it: the idea of God is the idea of a being who possesses all perfections. If such a being were not to exist it would lack the perfection of existence. Therefore the perfect being not only exists, but must exist; its non-existence would involve a contradiction.

That some philosophers consider the existence of God a matter for empirical decision, while others regard it as soluble by attention to meanings, is a point of considerable embarrassment to those who work in this area. So is the fact that some of the so-called empirical arguments are in important respects not empirical at all. But instead of discussing these matters further now, I shall proceed to the question how far the different proofs are convincing.

I begin with the Ontological Argument, since it is obvious that if it succeeds all other proofs are superfluous. Does it succeed? It must be confessed that though it has had distinguished supporters, the majority of philosophers have been inclined to treat it as no more than an ingenious quibble. As Kant first made clear, it trades on the idea that existence is a 'perfection' or quality like any other, as if the two sentences 'God is merciful' and 'God is existent' were of the same logical form. But it is easy enough to show that they are not. Compare on the one hand the idea of a God who is merciful with that of a God who is not merciful (the God of Thomas Hardy, for instance); compare on the other the idea of a God who exists with that of a God who does not exist. In the first case there is an obvious difference in the content of the two ideas: the merciful God and Hardy's God differ in conception at an all-important point. But when we turn to the second comparison the difference is not at all in the content, but in whether or not anything answers to the idea. A God who exists does not have an extra quality as against a God who does not exist; in idea he is exactly the same. David Hume puts this point by saying that whenever we think of something (for example, of the New Jerusalem) we think of it as existent, yet nothing follows from this about whether it exists in fact. This is not to say, of course, that questions about existence are unimportant; on the contrary, it is of supreme importance to determine whether or not there is a God. But the argument shows that the question cannot be settled, as St. Anselm and his followers supposed, by thinking as carefully as we can about what the term 'God' means or implies.

(The following two paragraphs may be omitted on a first reading.)

It has been argued by a contemporary American philosopher, Norman Malcolm, that this criticism, though valid against some versions of the Ontological Proof, do not touch its central contention, which is that God possesses the special property of *necessary* existence. The idea of God, as shown for example in the language of the Psalms, is that of a being which exists from everlasting to everlasting; it makes no sense to say of God that he came into existence at a particular point of time, or to speculate on the possibility of his ceasing to exist. In this respect the case of God is different from that of anything finite, which means that the comparisons made by critics of the Proof (for example by Kant when he likened God existing in fact or only in idea to a hundred dollars existing in fact or only in idea) are irrelevant. Malcolm maintains that the only question we have to face here is whether the concept of a being which possesses necessary existence is free of internal contradiction. If it is—and Malcolm thinks there is every reason to suppose that it is—God must exist as a matter of conceptual necessity.

Yet it seems that the argument in this version is open to precisely the same criticism as in the form previously considered. From the fact that I think of God as existent it cannot be inferred that he really exists; all that can be inferred is that if he exists, he exists. Similarly from the fact that I think of God as possessing the peculiar property of necessary existence, nothing can be inferred about his actual existence; the only legitimate conclusion is that if he exists, he possesses necessary existence. Malcolm objects to this criticism on the ground that it begs the question in the critics' favour, by talking of 'actual existence' and equating this with existence in space and time; he reminds us that we impose no such condition in discussing the existence of numbers, and insists that religious discourse too is an independent area of linguistic activity, which can claim legitimacy just because it is constantly used. But this comparison, though suggestive, is perhaps not completely convincing. As was mentioned earlier, the whole question of existence in mathematics is difficult; it could be that numbers exist only in some derivative or shadowy sense, one which believers would not regard as sufficiently full-blooded to suit the case of God. And apart from this, religion is at best a more controversial region than mathematics: to say that we must treat it as a going concern is to forget not only its enemies but, more important, those who view it with indifference and find its formulae lacking in real significance. To go through life ignoring mathematics in this kind of way would scarcely be possible.

The attraction of the Ontological Argument, as Descartes saw, is that if successful its conclusion is as certain as any conclusion in geometry. The same certainty cannot be claimed for any suggested empirical proof of God's existence, though the First Cause argument may seem to possess it, thanks to the extremely obvious character of the premiss from which it starts. As expounded above, the argument was that if something exists, something necessary must exist also, and this something necessary will be God; something contingent does exist, and therefore God exists. I have already explained that 'contingent' in this connexion means 'causally dependent'; I am, in this language, a contingent being because I owe my existence to my parents. But they in their turn are or were contingent because not self-produced; and the same is in fact true of everyone and everything in the world. There is no single constituent of the universe which does not refer away to something else as its cause. Yet (and here we come to the crux of the argument) the situation seems unintelligible if the reference continues without any limit. A series of things can lean one on another provided it terminates in something which stands up for itself, without being dependent on anything further. The claim of the First Cause argument is that the series of contingent beings must similarly terminate in something of a different order altogether, and that this will be the necessary being, God.

It may help to make this difficult line of thought more comprehensible if I mention at this point that it is sometimes presented in terms of *events* or *happenings* rather than, as above, in terms of *existents*. That something happens in the world is, we suppose, always the result of something which happened previously, and this in turn came about because of some preceding event. Whatever occurs is thus determined by some preceding event, which is in exactly the same case itself. Now the question arises can we suppose that the chain of antecedent causes stretches back *ad infinitum*? And there is an immediate impulse to answer this question in the negative, since after all we are dealing with something that has actually come about, which means that the conditions of its coming about must be complete. How they could be complete if they were also unlimited in number is not obvious. But if they are not unlimited the first member of the series must be different from all the others in a most important respect: whereas they were all conditioned by something previous to them, it will not point beyond itself but will be unconditioned. Again, whereas they will each occur at a determinate point in time, it must be thought of as lying outside time altogether. It will originate events in time, without being such an event itself.

We must now attempt to estimate the cogency of this case. To begin with, let us fasten attention on a notion which was central in both versions of the argument, the notion of causal dependence. We said that every contingent thing depended for its existence on something else, and again that every event was causally conditioned by some previous event. Now these two cases are less divergent than they may seem, for to say that one thing depends on another is to say that it is affected by what the other does. To speak more generally, it is happenings in things which are causally efficacious. In investigating the notion of causal dependence we can therefore concentrate on its application to happenings or events.

What conditions have to be satisfied if one event is to be pronounced the cause, or a case, of another? Hume argued persuasively that one condition which is necessary is that events of the first kind should be regularly followed by events of the second kind. Causality is a relationship not so much between single events as between types of events; or rather, it is a relationship between individual events in virtue of their general characteristics. And of course every event is a happening in time. To accept these doctrines is at once to set limits to the sphere of possible causal inferences. If Hume is right, we obviously cannot use a causal argument to establish the existence or properties of anything which transcends time altogether, nor again can we proceed by causal means to the conclusion that there exists a being totally unlike anything that has fallen within human experience. Yet both these moves are attempted in the First Cause argument for God's existence.

The reader may well think this criticism unfair: to say that the relation between God and the world cannot be understood in the terms we use to understand the connexion of things or events in the world is to say nothing which the theist would want to deny. But the difficulty for the latter is that of making clear the special relation of causal dependence on which his reasoning rests. One suggestion often made is that it should be seen as a relationship of ground and consequence: God's activities are not so much the cause of the world as its ground. However, it is ideas or propositions (for example, the propositions of a geometrical system) which are related as grounds to consequents; this is a logical rather than a factual relation, and it is not clear that it can be applied meaningfully to the sphere of existence. Nor will it do to take the easy way out and proclaim that God's relationship to the world is unique, at least if our aim is to argue from the world to God. On this subject at least the theist still has much to clarify.

(The following two paragraphs may be omitted on a first reading.)

It remains to say something on the central point of strength in the First Cause argument, the contention that we have to choose between an uncaused cause and a series of happenings (or existents) which is at once completed and infinite, the implication being, of course, that the second alternative can be ruled out as impossible. Here the answer may be along lines suggested by Kant, that we should think of the term 'cause' as belonging primarily to the vocabulary of explanation rather than that of description, with the result that causes are seen as conditions established in a regress argument rather than independently existing states of affairs. On this view we proceed backwards from an event to its causes instead of thinking that the latter must already be there for the event to occur; the advantage of the view as regards the present problem is that it enables us to avoid the dilemma which the First Cause theorist offers. For though it is the case that whatever cause we arrive at we can always take the causal enquiry further, we need not say either that infinitely many events must have preceded the event with which we deal or that the series must originate in a first uncaused cause. The field of causes will be indefinitely extendible, and thus neither finite nor infinite.

Whether these ideas can be accepted or not (and it is only

fair to mention that they are associated with a general account of the status of the familiar world which many philosophers reject), it must be pointed out that supporters of the First Cause argument have a special problem of their own, in the step where they identify with God the something necessary they conclude to exist. On this point too Kant had some shrewd observations to make. Let it be granted, he said, that the existence of contingent being implies that of necessary being: how do we make out that this necessary being must be God? We can do so only if we can assume the complex principle that if anything is a necessary being it has the characteristics of God, and if anything has the characteristics of God it is a necessary being. But the second half of this principle is precisely what was contended for in the Ontological Argument. Thus the First Cause proof can proceed to its conclusion only if its supporters accept the validity of the Ontological Proof, a step which few of them are willing to take.

I shall now comment on the Argument from Design, which has always had a special and widespread appeal. What gives it its attraction is that it depends on no profound subtleties but makes its point clearly and simply. There are, its supporters believe, central features of human experience which can be accounted for in one way only: by the hypothesis that the world was created by God. No one can deny that nature is orderly: the reign of natural law is unbroken, the fundamental simplicity of the universe (the fact that it can be understood in terms of relatively few principles which are systematically related) altogether greater than we should expect if it were the product of chance. Add to this the way in which the different parts of the physical and, still more, the biological world go together to form a marvellous economy, and it seems impossible to deny that the whole thing is the work of a supreme intelligence.

Yet there are overwhelming difficulties in the way of accepting this as a satisfactory argument. A sceptic could begin by disputing its very premisses: the world shows evidence of remarkable order, but it is also in some respects conspicuously lacking in order—think of the struggle for existence between different animal species in this connexion. Again, it is not true that we can assume, as many eighteenth-century writers did, that those parts of nature which apparently work together to promote some end are in fact the product of design: modern biologists and physiologists tend to explain the facts here as resulting from mechanical causes. Nor if these difficulties are ignored is the rest of the argument free of controversy. The most it can prove, even when taken on its own terms, is, as both Hume and Kant pointed out, that the universe was *ordered* by an intelligent being, as opposed to *created* by such a being: there is nothing in the case as stated to show that the material of the universe must have had any particular origin. The Argument from Design thus at best leads us to conclude that the world had a supreme architect. But we go too far if on the evidence of this argument alone we ascribe to this architect the qualities involved in the common philosophical concept of God, as illustrated in the quotation from Descartes given above. The world shows evidence of remarkable order, and its architect can hence be credited with remarkable powers. But it is one thing to say this, and another altogether to conclude that his powers are without limit: that he is omniscient, omnipotent, wholly self-subsistent, and so on. In so far as the argument is genuinely empirical, it gives no warrant for such a conclusion, and so fails to prove the existence of God.

Hume made a further point, to which reference has already been made, which he thought of special importance in connexion with this argument. The point can be made clear as follows. Suppose a sailor lands on a remote island and finds human footprints in the sand: he concludes that a human being has been there in the comparatively recent past. But he is able to make this inference because he has come across, or heard of, other instances of this phenomenon: neither effect nor cause is unique as far as he is concerned. In arguing causally he is proceeding, as was explained earlier, from one type of thing to another. But the supporter of the Argument from Design, who seeks to go from particular facts about the world to the existence of God, is in a very different position, since he wants to show that the facts can be accounted for only by postulating *the* intelligent being which is God; to stop at *some* intelligent being is not enough for him. When we reflect on Hume's point it becomes clear that in this respect at least the argument is bound to fail. Only if we are in a position to supply a supplementary premiss to the effect that no other intelligent being than God can be the cause in question, could we find it convincing. But we should not be warranted in supplying such a premiss unless God's existence were already certain on other grounds.

Theistically-minded philosophers have picked out widely different features of experience as explicable only on the hypothesis of God's existence. They have referred under this head to, among other things, the fact that we can form the idea of God at all; the fact that it is an idea familiar to all sorts and conditions of men, found in all cultures; the fact that we have notions of right and wrong, with a conscience which brings them to bear on our conduct; our ability to form value judgements generally; the enjoyment by human beings of certain special types of experience, aesthetic, religious and mystical above all others. But it is not necessary to examine each of these arguments individually to see that it is open to very much the same objections as have just been brought against the Argument from Design. Apart from the general troubles which beset any causal proof which attempts to go beyond the limits of experience, the conclusion which the propounder of the proof seeks to draw from his premisses is in every case more ambitious than they warrant. Collectively, the arguments may lend colour to a presumption: what they cannot do, whether individually or together, is to constitute a demonstration whose conclusion is unshakeable. Yet it was to find such a basis of certainty that the philosophical theologian or theistically-minded philosopher set out.

What lesson are we to draw from this largely negative discussion? I shall conclude by mentioning two lessons that have been suggested, and shall then refer briefly to a third possibility.

According to one group of philosophers, the Logical Positivists, the total failure of the traditional philosophical proofs of God's existence, together with the fact that no decisive considerations can be adduced on the other side, shows that the problem itself is a bogus one. These critics draw a sharp distinction between scientific questions, which are soluble by direct observation, by applying accepted laws and formulae or by forming a new theory and experimentally verifying its consequences, and metaphysical questions, which are not soluble by these methods. A metaphysical question is the product of thinking which is irretrievably muddled, and the only thing to do with it is to drop it as entirely unprofitable. That this analysis applies in the case we have examined, the critics would maintain on the ground that the arguments are, as we pointed out, neither straightforwardly empirical, as are arguments in history and to a large extent in the sciences, nor straightforwardly non-empirical, as are arguments in mathematics. They sometimes look empirical, but in every case can reach their conclusion only if unwarranted premisses of a non-empirical sort are brought in to supplement them. And they are unsatisfactory, the critics contend, in another way also: in that the entity they purport to discuss lies altogether beyond the range of experience. Since the infinite being is, by definition, utterly different from the things of this world, nothing we know about this world can count decisively either for or against the proposition that he exists. But in these circumstances it must be confessed that those who talk about such a being use words without meaning. The name 'God' on this view is a term without significance.

To adopt this criticism is to be committed to holding that theism (and atheism too) is not so much false as literally meaningless. Only science, in a broad sense of that term, makes sense, and neither theology nor religion, which produces theology's raw material, falls within the province of science. I cannot discuss here the many difficulties involved in this extreme, but nonetheless perennially attractive, position: it must suffice to mention that other philosophers have found much to criticise in its all too simple concept of meaning. The relevance of their criticisms to the present discussion may come out if we turn to the second suggested lesson.

Here we have to do with the reactions not of anti-metaphysical philosophers, but of persons who take religion seriously. There are many believers who are not disconcerted when they learn that attempts to construct a rational proof of the existence of God are one and all unsuccessful; this failure on the part of philosophical theology seems to them to leave their own activities untouched. Religion, they feel, is a matter of immediate conviction rather than argument; as Kierkegaard said, the man who looks for logical demonstrations in this area shows that he has utterly failed to understand it. The sphere of faith is entirely separate from that of reason. This seems, on the face of it, to make religious belief completely irrational, but the unpalatability of that view is lessened when it is added, as it is by a number of contemporary philosophers sympathetic to this attitude, that religious discourse has its own internal logic. Logical Positivists were right in arguing that statements about God do not make sense in the way statements in science or mathematics do; it does not follow, however, that they make no sense at all. That they are significant for the believer is obvious from the fact that religion is a matter of corporate practice in which many persons engage; that these persons understand each other when they use the name 'God' is very hard to deny. So if we want proof of God's existence the proper place to look is the writings and sayings of religious men, and the proper evidence to adduce their use of sentences like 'I know that my Redeemer liveth'. It is here that the concept of God is a living reality rather than a mere corpse for dissection by philosophers.

The trouble with this solution is that while it may satisfy the person who is wholly absorbed in religious practice, it can do little to help the doubter and nothing for the man who stands outside religion altogether. This is because it can no longer claim that religion is a source of objective knowledge; for it, religious truth must be purely internal and not to be judged by the standards of science or everyday life. Admittedly, scientific and even mathematical truth would no longer be universal and objective if the philosophical sympathisers we have mentioned took their view to its logical conclusion; but this shows not the strength but the weakness of the attempt to claim that a type of discourse can have its own logic and truth. Whatever may be the case with the simple and unquestioning believer, reflective persons can scarcely be satisfied to leave the matter there.

Is there a third alternative? I think myself that there is, though I can sketch it only very briefly here and cannot attempt to estimate its tenability. To introduce it let me recur to a phrase used a page or two back about the traditional arguments lending colour to a presumption. It seems natural to think that when an argument fails to establish its point with complete certainty, it can nevertheless show that it possesses some degree of probability. Some philosophers and theologians, including Pascal and Bishop Butler in his famous work *The Analogy of Religion*, have held that God's existence is a matter of reasonable probability. It is clear, however, that the critics of reason's pretensions who formulated the other two views would be no more content with this position than with that of the discredited metaphysician; they would find the same difficulty in admitting rational belief as in allowing knowledge here. It might nevertheless be possible to get round their objections if the suggestion were made that we take the different arguments as illustrating and supporting an overall view of the world, one which sees everything that there is as permeated by divinity. To make this intelligible, consider an alternative overall theory which is widely current today: the thesis of materialism. Supporters of this thesis hold that, in the end, everything can be satisfactorily explained in material or natural terms; there is no need to appeal to anything supernatural or spiritual to account either for the world of nature or for the world of men. Against this there have been many thinkers who have taken what might be called a religious-centred rather than a scientifically-centred view of the world, and have maintained that natural categories are totally inadequate for the understanding of many aspects of our experience. Their case for dismissing materialism is made by pointing to much the same phenomena as are mentioned by supporters of the traditional theistic arguments: the order of the universe, the spiritual and moral strivings of man, the ubiquity of the idea of God, and so on. It is on this evidence that they conclude that the world in which we live is not merely natural. And though they would have to admit that no compelling reasons can be advanced in support of this contention, they would claim that the same was true of its rival or rivals. When we deal with theses of this generality it is perhaps too much to hope for definite decisions for or against. But this will not show that all discussion of such theses must be abandoned as senseless, as the Logical Positivists suggested. The very fact that materialism remains a live issue is enough to prove that the case for a theistic form of metaphysics cannot be dismissed out of hand.

4
Moral Philosophy

R. W. Hepburn

General Account of the Subject

Some parts of philosophy are difficult to introduce, because the questions they are concerned with do not normally arise in everyday life. We are not ordinarily perplexed about the correct account of entailment or negation, or about how to justify our belief that other people have minds. The problems of moral philosophy, however, are more familiar. Not only are we often perplexed about where our duty lies in particular situations, but we are at least occasionally perplexed about the more general question—how can we reliably make *any* judgement about right and wrong, good and bad? How can we tell when a debate over right and wrong has been won or lost: what are the marks of success or failure? They are by no means obvious. What has to be done, in order to prove that some activity is morally despicable, that one trait of character is a vice and another a virtue? Is reasoning in this field at all like reasoning in science, in criticism of the arts, or in chess? Is reasoning the vital factor, anyway? or is morality more a matter of how people *feel,* of what they (or their societies) happen to approve or disapprove of, or of how they react? Again, when a person is confronted by a duty he would much rather not acknowledge, he is liable to ask why he should take this or any other duty seriously; why let himself be fenced in by obligations that can be very costly to fulfil. What is the source of their authority—parental orders, social pressures, divine commandments . . . ?

All these general problems, and many more related to

them, are germane to moral philosophy. In fact, the moral philosopher could be described simply as the person who perseveres with the probing of such problems beyond the point where they become complex and elusive and are usually abandoned.

Let us look at his tasks in a slightly less random way, beginning with the most particularised problems and going on to the more abstract and general. At the former end of this scale lie practical problems about what John Smith ought to do in a particular dilemma. (Ought he, for instance, to confess that his prosperous and now honestly-run business was founded on a dishonest deal years ago? If he tells, his wife and children stand to suffer as well as he.) Giving advice about such dilemmas is not normally seen as part of the philosopher's task, although his work can certainly be of indirect help by clarifying the issues and the forms of argument involved.

Suppose, however, in course of arguing out a particular moral problem, someone appealed to a *general test* of the rightness and wrongness of acts, then a philosopher could not deny that the scrutiny of such tests has formed part of his subject-matter—from Plato's day to the present. What would such a test look like? It might be one of the following:

(i) 'Which of the acts open to me would yield me most pleasure?' Here attention centres upon the gratification of the doer of the act, the individual moral agent himself. Such an account is called an *egoistic* moral theory. To say that it is the agent's *pleasure* or *happiness* that moral action seeks to increase, makes the theory also a form of 'hedonism' (from Greek, *hēdonē*, pleasure).

(ii) 'Which act would most closely conform to the conventions, the standard practices, of my society or of my class within society?' That is to say, I may consider not the effects of an act upon my own weal or woe, but its agreement with 'what's done and what's not done' in a social group with which I am identified.

(iii) 'Which of the act open to me would do most to increase the happiness (or reduce the suffering) of the largest number of people?' Again we should be primarily concerned with the *consequences* of actions (and the consequences for pleasure or pain). A much wider range of consequences would be relevant than in test (i). As in test (ii), we are concerned with society; but test (iii) might conceivably counsel the breaking of a convention or standard practice, if the welfare of society would be furthered by so doing.

(iv) 'Which of the acts open to me would conform to the will, or commands, of God?' Here attention would be focused, not primarily upon the well-being of oneself or others affected by one's act, not upon human *mores*, but upon a supremely authoritative divine imperative.

In the second part of this chapter I shall explore the strengths and weaknesses of certain of these tests—if only in a preliminary way. Here I simply list them, as four out of a great many attempts to sum up all moral requirements in a single formula. Nonetheless, merely to list them has made it clear that the various tests could yield conflicting answers to the question 'What ought I to do?'. For instance, tests (ii), (iii) and (iv) allow that moral demands may involve the sacrificing of my individual happiness; but test (i) does not. And some alleged divine commands (e.g. that Abraham should slay Isaac) clash with non-religious conceptions of right and wrong.

Some of the moral philosopher's problems, then, are problems about what characteristics may be shared by our various duties or ideals—whether they all make for happiness, or involve obedience to God, and so on. But other problems in this field are not so much about the content of morality as about *the way we come to know* what is right or wrong, good or bad. We have already seen this topic looming up. For an example: we could not come to know that an unprovoked killing is wrong, simply by inspecting the scene of the crime, remarking upon the bullet-holes, the inertness of the deceased, and so on. The 'wrongness' is not a feature of the situation that we can handle, see or photograph: not an observable fact among other facts. What are we doing then, when we pronounce, confidently enough, that a wicked deed has been done? If we are not seeing, touching, hearing the wickedness (but still wish to say we are *apprehending* it somehow), shall we say we are 'intuiting' it? that a moral quality is a quality not perceptible by the senses, known only by intuition? That kind of answer has indeed been often suggested.

On the other hand, there is a kind of philosopher who finds that answer profoundly unsatisfying. 'The perceiving of a quality by intuition'—this (he will say) is in fact a grandiose, inflated misdescription of our moral reactions. It *looks* as if something important is being said, but once all the qualifications are made ('you cannot *see* the quality, *touch* or *hear* it . . .'), there is only the ghost of a quality left. And why should the presence of such a pseudo-quality exert any practical pressure upon us—as moral judgements *do* exert pressures in our lives? So now he suggests an alternative theory. Our moral judgements (he claims) are reports upon our feelings, upon our revulsion at the killing, upon our delight at a generous act, and so on. There is no more problem about how we know in moral matters than there is over how we know our own feelings, emotions and attitudes.

Commonsensical and tidy. But again it needs to be asked —does that theory, attractive though it is, have any (less obvious) implications that are unwelcome and unplausible? Again it is possible to draw at least one such implication. This theory makes nonsense of moral *disputes*. If Smith claims that it was morally justifiable to use the A-bomb on Hiroshima, and Jones says it was *un*justifiable, we understand them to be contradicting each other. But on this 'inner report' theory, they are not contradicting each other at all. Smith is reporting upon the feelings within him, and Jones is reporting upon the feelings Jones has. In order to contradict Smith, Jones would have to say, 'No: you have misdescribed your feelings: you really feel disapproval'. This certainly seems to caricature moral disagreement, and thus to call in question any theory that has such consequences.

It is possible to shift ground, in the following way. Moral judgements perhaps do not *report* upon inner feelings and responses, but they *express* these reactions, nevertheless. 'That was a difficult and dangerous act to perform' could be understood as only a more discriminating version of 'Bravo!'

Now, if our main model of moral judgement were an *exclamatory* one, what would happen to the problem about moral disagreement and contradiction? You cannot have contradiction, if nothing has been *asserted*; and on this theory we replace assertions by exclamations. Even so, Smith and Jones could still clash over Hiroshima—by expressing opposite *attitudes* to what was done.

Or yet again, it may be argued that the language of exclamations and interjections is not as close to that of moral discourse as is the language of commands, imperatives. To urge that an act *ought* to be done, or that such and such is the *best* policy, is not far from saying '*Do* that act; *Adopt* that policy'. And moral disagreement? On an Imperative account, disagreements would be like conflicting orders: 'Do *X*'. 'No don't; do *Y* instead'.

We cannot take this story further, except to say that both exclamatory and imperative theories may find it difficult to account fully for the place of reason and argument in the moral life. We do not simply say, '*X* is right', '*Y* is the worst of the alternatives'. We give reasons for moral judgements; many of our judgements, if not all, are connected by threads of logical relationship. They are not discrete interjections or isolated commands.

Can justice be done to this side of morality, while retaining any of the models we have been reviewing?

Looking back over the last few pages, you will see that we have travelled a long way, very rapidly. We started by mentioning particular practical moral quandaries—that lie on the threshold of moral philosophy; and our direction of travel has been towards the more general and comprehensive. On the way, we have noted the question about touchstones of moral value, and the question about the sorts of knowing or perceiving or feeling that are involved in moral judgement. These questions are in fact all interconnected; and in touching upon the last of these themes, we have touched also upon questions more general still. 'What sort of judgement is a moral judgement?' and 'What sort of concepts are moral concepts?' Moral philosophy cannot afford to work in a vacuum; it has to compare moral judgements with other kinds of judgements—judgements of taste, judgements about works of art, judgements in geometry, judgements in the field of law. It must compare and contrast the concepts of morals with the concepts of science and of mathematics. When it discusses the justification of punishment by the state, it can hardly ignore what jurists and criminologists have to say. When it studies the concepts of rights and of liberty, it overlaps with social and political philosophy. We have seen already that it can have liaisons with theology; and we shall note later on that it can learn also from psychology and imaginative literature.

A further range of problems needs at least to be mentioned in this introductory outline. These are problems not about the criteria of right and wrong action, and not about the concepts used in moral appraisal, but about the moral agent himself. Under what conditions, we have to ask, is a living being morally responsible? Neither a sheep nor a very young child is held morally responsible, nor again an adult whose sanity is radically impaired. But what is it about human beings generally that does give them moral status? 'Rationality' will be part of the answer—though the word does not tell us much without a long elucidation. 'Freedom' will be another vital (and connected) answer. A man is responsible only if he is free: moral appraisal *presupposes* freedom. But freedom from *what*? That question is the overture to yet another debate.

Finally, it is worth returning to a topic, so far just alluded to but brushed aside. What is the relation between moral theory and moral *practice*? If the moral philosopher is not a moral adviser, a counsellor over quandaries of practical choice, do his enquiries have no bearing *at all* upon the practical perplexities of everyday life? If so, his activity must surely seem unattractively remote and esoteric. In fact, to say they have no bearing is to exaggerate just as much as to see them as furnishing a moral ready-reckoner. For, even if moral philosophy should fail to discover any relatively simple touchstone of moral value, it certainly can and does show up the irrelevance and unreliability of many 'touchstones' that people actually apply in practical moral perplexities. Part of its task, that is, is to offer a continuing critique of moral assumptions, slogans, recipes, programmes: a task that can undoubtedly affect moral practice in the end. When it contrasts the forms of moral argumentation with reasoning in other fields and disciplines, this too can have practical relevance. It can warn us against trying to reach moral conclusions by inappropriate methods, and against rejecting a moral argument simply because it does not conform to the pattern of argument in (say) geometry or physics.

Summing up: moral decisions, often of great importance, are often made in a haze of muddle and incomprehension about the nature of what is being done. Although the moral philosopher is no oracle, he does exert himself to reduce that haze, to enable moral deliberation to be carried on in a more rational and clear-sighted manner.

It is, in any case, artificial and misleading to make a sharp separation between practical moral deliberation and moral theory. Certain trains of reflection, for instance, can make a person wonder whether the entire moral enterprise has not something delusory about it. Suppose he comes to consider his brain as a complex electrochemical mechanism, and he wonders whether it makes sense any more to speak of being creative or free, as a moral agent is required to be free. He reads Freud, and he wonders whether 'conscience' can have the solemn authority it once seemed to have. He is perplexed over the mortality or immortality of his soul; and he wonders whether, if this life is all we have, morality can keep its seriousness for him. These perplexities are both practical and theoretical issues. They are clearly theoretical (about how we are to understand freedom, how to relate 'conscience' to 'super-ego', how to relate moral valuation to the thought of death and annihilation). But they are no less clearly practical, in that each of them seems to contain a threat to our status as moral agents, threatens to undermine in some way our general moral seriousness or moral stamina.

In the first of the extended illustrations that now follow, we can sample in a little more detail the sorts of argument moral philosophers conduct over the question of a single touchstone of right and wrong, good and bad. In the second we shall sample the debate over what is probably the chief presupposition of morality—the freedom of the will.

One Moral Goal, or Many Duties . . . ?

We have seen that one of the most natural questions to ask when reflecting about morality is: 'What is the ultimate goal or objective of moral endeavour?' or 'What are we trying to achieve when we perform duties and aspire after moral ideals?' Let us start again with that question.

Natural though it be, the question may meet a rebuff. 'You know well enough what the moral life is like;' someone may say, 'it does not have any single objective. It involves a vast variety of obligations to act and not act in particular ways: to keep promises, not to tell lies, to develop one's talents, but not to steal or assault: to foster certain traits of character (like sincerity and conscientiousness) and to extirpate others (like greed, envy and sloth).'

The complexity is daunting, but it should not choke off the question: can some unity be yet concealed behind the diversity? After all, the rules of a tennis club are also diversified; they include rules about permitted footwear, about the paying of subscriptions and about hours of permitted play. Despite the diversity they clearly do have a single aim—to facilitate the playing of tennis by members. So too with rules and regulations in a school or university. These would lose all *raison d'être* but for the goal of education—even though some of the rules do not advance that goal in the most direct and immediate way. (Fire-precaution rules or library-rules, for instance.)

Anyway, people do tend to assume that morality also has some single point, despite *its* diversity. Its point is 'To keep society going', or 'To avoid social chaos', or 'To give people a chance to live as they want to live', or 'To realise a way of life centred uniquely upon Christian love'.

Earlier we remarked that such accounts can be embarrassingly numerous and conflicting. To detect conflict, however, does not by itself help us to sort out the reliable from the unreliable accounts. How do we sort them out? One obvious question, for any formula, is: 'Does it cover all the cases, unify all our obligations?' Society, for instance, could be 'kept going', chaos kept at bay, even though quite a number of moral principles were ignored, and some others only perfunctorily obeyed. A theory of that sort could account only for the few basic principles without which a community could scarcely exist: respect for the life and possessions of others, readiness not to pursue personal retaliation when wronged, and the like. Important though these are, they are not the whole of morality.

It may seem more plausible to claim that the whole of morality is a living out of what the New Testament calls *agapē*, love. This claim, however, needs to be elucidated. To act out of love involves very different acts in different situations. Love makes different demands upon a person when he is acting towards, for instance, his wife, his children, his employer, his customers, clients or pupils. And in reckoning with these differences, we cannot avoid bringing back that complex of rules and principles that we hoped the reference to love might simplify. Furthermore, there can be poignant conflicts between the requirements of love and the requirements of *justice*. If in some circumstances it is difficult to satisfy both, this strongly suggests that love cannot be the only basic moral principle.

To sum up so far. In our reflecting upon morality, there tends to be an oscillation between two poles. We are sometimes struck by the multiplicity and variety of our duties; they seem a bewildering and unconnected assortment. But then we probe for any possible hidden connexions. We seem to find some. We leap to a general formula from which all duties and all moral ideals can be derived. Then we (or our critics) test the formula against some awkward cases, and it may fail. Nevertheless, we can learn a great deal about the nature of morality, just as the engineer learns about his materials and experimental structures by testing them 'to destruction'.

It is important to notice that we do not simply have a multiplicity of moral goals, each of roughly the same type or form. To talk about goals is to talk about ends of action, about the states of affairs we are seeking to bring about through our action. Some moral principles, however, do not seem to be primarily about goals, ends or consequences to be achieved. They seem to look back rather than forward. Think of contracts and promises. A promise binds me, because of words said or written in the past: 'I promise to subscribe', 'You can count on my help'. Once the promise is made, it is not the anticipated results of keeping it, the unhappy consequences of *not* keeping it, that exert the moral pressure. Furthermore, certain special relationships between people seem able to generate duties and rights, again without the chief or obvious concern being with consequences or moral objectives. If I stand to someone as parent to child or husband to wife, a range of particular duties arises precisely from that relationship itself.

So it looks as if there may be at least two different sources of the multiplicity that we have remarked upon. First, the goals of moral action may be plural; and secondly, we may have some duties and some rights that are not at all obviously concerned with attaining these goals. Sometimes the question is: 'Which of the acts open to me would bring about the best, most valuable consequences?' But in other situations the question is: 'Did I promise?' or 'Is it just; is it fair?'

Nevertheless, many philosophers have argued that *despite* this appearance of complexity, morality is basically about the production of some single valuable state of affairs—such as the general happiness or the furthering of evolutionary progress. They argue that those obligations (like promise-keeping) which do not seem to fit the pattern, can nevertheless be shown to do so indirectly. Without promise-keeping, for instance, there would not be confidence between people in their co-operative tasks; and co-operation is required for most human endeavours. These theories that try to account for the whole range of moral ideals, duties and rights in terms of a goal or goals, are called 'teleological' theories (Greek, *telos*, end or objective). Opposing theories will argue that in some cases the last word has to be: 'It is just my duty to . . . (to refuse the dishonest deal, to return the loan which the lender has forgotten about . . .)'. And such a theory, giving an ultimate place to duty, can be called a 'deontological' theory (Greek, *deon*, necessary or binding).

For a specimen of the debate between these types of view, let us pursue, for a few pages at least, the question: 'Can we work out a convincing teleological theory in which the forms of goodness are claimed to be ultimately one?'

One version of such a theory, repeatedly offered from ancient times to the present (and mentioned above, p. 94), argues that the moral objective is the advantage of the moral agent himself. It would be unreasonable, that is, to submit oneself to the restriction of moral rules, unless it were to one's individual advantage to do so—in the long run, if not in every short run. If I am considering whether or not to join a sports club or to enrol in a college, I ask myself what advantage joining or enrolling would bring me. Once committed, I shall be under various rules relating to members or to students: but I put myself under these rules only if I first see some prospect of profit, enjoyment or other gain in the enterprise—whether of play or of study. Both game-playing and study can involve hard effort, fatigue or anxiety: but I anticipate that the rewards and satisfactions will outweigh these—or else, again, I should not join or enrol. Is it not the same with the entire *moral* enterprise—even though in its case there is no formal joining? To make the suggestion is easy enough; the harder task is to show in detail that the moral life actually is the gratifying or happy or profitable life for the person who leads it. It has to be shown that self-concern is not opposed to morality, but, instead, is its essence.

A dramatic, simplifying move may be made at this point. Self-concern, it may be said, cannot be blameworthy—for the reason that all human action is, *and must be*, done out of self-concern. Without the prospect of some gratification, a human being cannot be stirred to action at all. Only desire can initiate action; and desire comes into being only if some good for oneself is anticipated. The theory may be given at least an appearance of scientific status. Action occurs only if some 'drive', instinctual or other, is present, and such drives work towards the reduction of pain or need, or else towards a gain in satisfactory experience. Suppose you try to produce some counter-evidence; say, a person who sacrifices a great part of his life's-savings in his efforts to have his brother's wrongful conviction quashed, and so clear his brother's name. It might be argued, nevertheless, that this person wanted the clearing of his brother's name more than he wanted anything else (more than money in the bank). It was this strongest desire that led him to act. He acted so as to *gratify* that desire. We are not, that is, outside the circle of 'psychological egoism' (as this theory is usually labelled).

It is fairly easy to convert someone, temporarily at least, to egoism. Even so, the convert is likely to feel that 'something must be wrong with the theory somewhere'. How, for instance, can we see a morally self-sacrificing action as *praiseworthy* any more, if it is really an exercise in self-gratification, self-fulfilment? And something seems distorted about the picture of human action with which the theory works. It is true that only the enticement of some reward for the agent can prompt his action?

We may wish, for instance, to say that one human being can certainly act out of concern for another's welfare; and we may be convinced of that far more surely than we are convinced by the arguments of the theory. But we have still to show where the theory goes wrong. For a start, let us develop the point just made. We can recognise cases when we do have a self-regarding eye on the plaudits of others or on enhanced self-esteem, but we are able to distinguish these from cases where we are not concerned with plaudits or self-esteem, but only with the act itself. For instance, we are giving aid to a car-accident victim, or rescuing an animal from rising floodwaters—disinterestedly, in both cases. Since this distinction is obliterated in the theory, does not that count against the theory? A man can disregard his appetites or inclinations, whichever way they point, and do what ought to be done, simply *because* it ought.

Then, says the egoist, *that* is what he most wants to do . . . The distinction as we presented it *needs* to be obliterated. How do we reply?

First, there must be a closer look at the word 'want'. In one sense it is true that a person acts only if he wants to. But in this (weak) sense we are saying no more than that he *chooses* to act, that he is not compelled, manhandled. It does not follow that whatever he chooses to do is done so as to gratify himself. Again, a moral act may produce an incidental pleasure, sense of achievement, or peace of mind; but it does not follow that it was done *expressly to obtain* that reward.

An objector may retort, 'That is a noble and idealistic point of view, but people are not made like that. It is a scientific truth that the only spring of action is the prospect of some gratification for the agent.' Now this claim may be impressive and intimidating: but one ought not to let it intimidate. In fact, it may well turn out, when examined, not to be genuine science at all. In the first place, if someone presents what he claims is new information about the world, it is often useful (and always logically in order) to ask him what would be evidence *against* it. The point is not whether in fact counter-evidence can be obtained, but what such evidence would be like. If no counter-evidence can even be *conceived*, then whatever the original claim was intended to be, it was not really a piece of information about the world.

Suppose J. J. finances his friend's holiday cruise, in order to help him to recover from a serious illness. Counter-evidence to psychological egoism? Of course not, we shall be told—the action is really selfish: his friend may not be well-off, but perhaps he has great influence with J. J.'s employer. But no: the friends have quite different professional associates. Then J. J. is avid for praise on account of this generous act. No, it turns out, he has been discreet, and the gift is a secret between him and his friends. Then, comes the reply, he must be motivated by a desire for self-satisfaction, self-approval. . . .

The tell-tale word in this last sentence is the word 'must'. It shows us that nothing whatever is going to be accepted as evidence against the psychological egoist account; that counter-evidence is inconceivable. If that is so, the theory loses its right to be called scientific, or even informative. Thus, no good grounds have been offered for not retaining what does seem given to us in experience, namely the distinction between self-regarding and other-regarding actions.

Psychological egoism might be false and yet other forms of egoism might be true. Even though it were *possible* for me to act simply for the sake of another person's good, it might never be my *duty* to do so. My sole duty might be a duty to further my own well-being, however that is conceived. Let us consider this possibility, very briefly.

To be an egoist in this sense does not entail that I should steal, lie or deceive, in order to advance my interests. I could argue that it is far more to my advantage to enjoy the pleasures of open and honest co-operation with others, and that egoism will actually counsel me to live by very much the same rules and principles as non-egoists live by.

Or is this a superficial account? Could there not very easily be a conflict between duty and self-interest, even long-term self-interest? For instance, in a totalitarian regime, a citizen may have a duty to disobey the state (to refuse, say, to assist in a political 'purge'), although he knows that the state will quickly and cruelly revenge itself upon him. It is one thing to claim that dutiful behaviour often happily coincides with the advantage of the agent: it is another thing to claim that it invariably does. In a word, it is absurd to deny the existence of moral self-sacrifice.

There are further difficulties. A person very often makes moral judgements about situations that do not affect him at all, where he has the prospect neither of advantage nor disadvantage. His judgements may nevertheless be confident—perhaps even passionate. They may relate to events in the remote past or events in the future whose outcome he will not be alive to enjoy or to suffer. Again, I may be quite undecided whether I stand to gain or to lose, say, if Smith breaks his contract with Jones. But uncertainty on that score may, once more, coexist in me with a perfectly confident moral judgement: Smith ought not to break his contract. So it does not look as if assessing the moral quality of a situation can be the same thing as assessing potential advantage or disadvantage to myself.

It may be answered that the question about Smith is whether it would be to *Smith*'s advantage to break his contract. This move would not save the theory. What do we mean by 'the question about Smith'? If Smith himself asks the question, 'Ought I . . .?', of course it is his own advantage he must consider, on the theory. But if I (as a spectator) ask the question about Smith—whose advantage ought I to consider? Could it be Smith's advantage? That would mean that I ought sometimes to consider the advantage of people other than myself; and this would be inconsistent with egoism.

The same considerations show that egoism makes nonsense of *moral advice*. If Smith asks me, 'Ought I break this contract?', I shall have to give the answer that will further my own (not Smith's) interests—if I am a consistent egoist. This information certainly is not what Smith means to elicit, by his question. Nor, if he consults a succession of advisers, will he expect to be told what each adviser would personally prefer him to do—so as to further that adviser's advantage.

Although, as usual, the argument could go on a great deal further, it does begin to look as if our obligations and ideals *cannot* be unified in the way egoism suggests, that they cannot be shown as really a single duty to advance the agent's welfare, happiness or interests. The interests of others are crucial in moral deliberation as we know it. This could of course be granted, and the search for a unifying principle continued. Could our duties to people at large be aspects of what is ultimately a single duty? We have already alluded to one such view—the view called 'hedonistic utilitarianism'. This is the claim that the goal of all moral endeavour is the greatest happiness of the greatest number of people. (All forms of *hedonism* claim that the sole ultimate value is pleasure or happiness. A *utilitarian* theory claims that one ought to maximise good at large—indeed, that morality *amounts* to this.) Faced with alternative possible actions, the clear-sighted moral agent asks, 'What action is most likely to realise the maximum happiness for the maximum number?' Morality, that is to say, is neither an affair of self-interest nor a mere blind obeying of principles that have no discernible point. Moral principles (about promise-keeping, truth-telling etc.) still retain their force within utilitarianism, but they derive that force from their ability to further the supreme goal.

Historically, hedonistic utilitarianism has played an important part in giving a theoretical grounding to various movements of social and moral reform. It is a powerful critical weapon against oppressive social institutions, laws or government policies. It demands that all these should be assessed simply and solely in terms of their effects upon the happiness of the individuals they touch.

Nonetheless, a moral theory can be valuable in practice and apply convincingly to a large range of moral phenomena, yet not be finally adequate over the whole range and not unify the whole field. In the present case it may be pointed out that our duty often is not to increase someone's happiness, but rather to decrease someone's suffering. To say that is not to quibble. Given a situation where we can either relieve misery or add to the happiness of someone already reasonably happy, priority clearly needs to be given to the first. This is not just because the same act of philanthropy (a gift of money say) would make a bigger difference to the state of the miserable person than to the state of the moderately happy man. The mere fact of the suffering gives an urgency to our concern with the sufferer that is quite absent from the other's case. The seemingly simple and single utilitarian principle begins to reveal signs of inadequacy.

It is easy to bring out further difficulties. Hedonism claims that there is only one form of value—pleasure or happiness. Yet, unless we use these words in a quite meaninglessly wide sense, they plainly do not cover the whole field of what is valuable or worthwhile for its own sake. The pursuit of knowledge, for instance, is not merely a search for ways of becoming contented and happy. Nor is it, as a search, always pleasurable or satisfying. The pursuit of knowledge may bring a good deal of disquiet, frustration and dissatisfaction—and yet may be chosen in preference to a life of unenquiring, complacent contentment. Again, certain human relationships, of friendship or love, can yield more anxiety, sometimes anguish, than pleasure overall. Yet we would hesitate to say that it would be better not to know friendship or love. We imply that these have a value independent of what hedonism can account for.

A poet or musician may suffer extreme dissatisfactions in the throes of composition, and yet believe that aesthetic creation is momentously valuable in its own right. He may say so independently of any calculating of pleasures and pains. When hedonism would award a 'minus' score, we may confidently insist on a 'plus'.

The ideal shows signs of fragmenting, so let us look away from it to the field of moral rules. Here the key question is this: can the utilitarian make good his claim that moral rules and principles are guiding rails and lane-markings towards the greatest happiness? It is true that some rules can be understood in this way plausibly enough: but it is very doubtful whether all can.

Suppose, for instance, that by torturing one prisoner, a commander could discover where a terrorist bomb has been planted, and thereby save several innocent people from injury and death. We could put up a strong utilitarian case for saying, 'Torture the prisoner'. But it might be said that this really brings out the inadequacy of the utilitarian principle. There are kinds of acts that simply ought not to be performed upon a human being, even if other people (perhaps greater in number) may benefit from them. Among such acts is the act of torturing. Any moral rule that forbids torturing would seem to require a grounding that utilitarianism cannot give it. On the other hand, it is possible (though we cannot go into this) that a defender of utilitarianism might say: 'Torture *can* be condemned on utilitarian grounds: and it *would* be condemned, if we fully realised the long-term effects on society of allowing the practice.'

Controversy has ranged over all those moral rules that are particularly concerned with *justice*. Suppose that some person or government greatly adds to the sum of happiness, in a family or in a nation; we still need to ask, in any moral review of what has been done—Was this good distributed *fairly*? And the question of fairness does look quite distinct from the question about quantity of good done.

The question of fairness enters again, and very obviously, if we try to explain on utilitarian lines the punishment of offenders by the state. Such an account can start easily enough. The objective of the state's action can be to *protect* the body of citizens from criminal acts; to *deter* potential criminals; to *reform* the persons immediately concerned. But a critic of utilitarianism will point out that something vital is missing from such an account—namely the notion of *guilt*. The wrongful arrest, 'rigged' trial and conviction of an innocent man might well deter real offenders, and by so doing protect the community. Again, that utilitarian account might justify a course of compulsory 'reform' for a person who had not (or not yet) committed any criminal act. It is only if we add the concept of guilt as essential to the idea of just punishment that we can bring the theory closer to ordinary beliefs. To add it, however, would once more show that utilitarianism has failed to unify all moral requirements into a single requirement—the promotion of the general happiness.

Utilitarians fight back—though it would take a substantial book to examine the possible replies and counter-replies. On guilt, for instance, they might urge the following. A state in which a person might at any time be tried and 'punished' without having committed a crime would be an anxiety-ridden, nightmare state, not an approach to a 'happy' state. So there are good utilitarian grounds for punishing the law-breaker, the guilty, only.

But, says the critic, if the practice of sometimes sentencing innocent people were a state secret, the utilitarian advantages would be obtained without the general nightmare. And yet the whole practice would still be radically unjust.

The reply comes: That sort of thing *cannot* be kept a secret: it inevitably leaks out.

Maybe, says the critic, but it is not the risk of leakage that makes the practice unjust: we use different principles (non-utilitarian ones) in judging it to be unjust, *whether it comes to be known or not*. And similar comments can be made about the utilitarian treatment of other obligations—where secrecy would prevent the unhappy effects, but would not prevent the action from being morally wrong.

Though we are, once more, about to break off the debate, it is only fair to add that utilitarian rejoinders to those criticisms are still possible. Here is just one: Many of those objections would be overcome if moral rules were seen not as mere rules of thumb, to be superseded whenever it seems expedient to supersede them, but as having a place of much greater authority in the scheme of morality. It is consummately important that people should be able to count upon the behaviour of others, i.e. that moral issues should, in the vast majority of cases, be rule-guided. The happiness or welfare of the community would be greatly harmed, not helped, if individuals reserved the right to calculate the gains and losses involved in the keeping of every promise or the telling of every true statement, and to decide on their action in accordance with the answer. The community's well-being is immensely benefited, if individuals *give up* that right and commit themselves to promise-keeping and to truth-telling as general practices. So we can respect the rules and remain utilitarians simultaneously.

Would this sort of defence allow the utilitarian to cope with all the difficulties we mentioned over justice and punishment?

Perhaps, it may be thought, unsatisfactory theories, such as egoism and utilitarianism, are unsatisfactory because they make no essential reference to a transcendent source of morality—that is, to *God*. Should we read their inadequacies as counselling us to turn back from man-fashioned moralities to a morality of the divine will? Let us consider very briefly the structure that such a will-of-God moral theory might have: its formal structure, not the particular content it might be given.

Doing what morality requires—the theory states—is a matter of acting in conformity with the will of God, as revealed in the canonical scriptures. God's command alone has moral authority. As it is by his creative *fiat* that we live at all, so it is only by his imperative that we can live *well*. . . .

Already, however, we can imagine someone objecting to such an account of morality, along these lines:

'I am not, for my part, convinced that any God exists, or, therefore, that there are any divine commands. Do you mean that I have no reason to pay any attention to right and wrong; that it does not matter if I am dishonest or cruel or . . . ?'

'No,' says the will-of-God moralist, 'I hope you will continue to be honest and kind—but your moral seriousness is really a fortunate carry-over from religious belief. You can't properly account for it, unless God does exist.'

'I cannot agree with that,' comes the reply, 'I can see that cruelty is wicked, without having to think about any God, real or imaginary. Besides, there is something very curious about your own claim. How do you know that to discover the will of God on some moral issue is to discover what is right and good?'

'Because God himself is good and his commands are right.'

'Then I ask you how you know *that*. Surely it must be because you have accepted certain accounts—mostly biblical ones—about God's nature and acts, and you have recognised in these accounts the signs of moral goodness and rightness. But, in order to *do* that, to recognise these, you must independently know what is good and right. Your "test" could not apply *there*—when you are asking whether the God of Old and New Testaments is worthy of worship and obedience. . . . So your test doesn't really tell us how *you* know good from bad, right from wrong, any more than it tells how *I* know these.'

I said that we should consider the formal structure of a will-of-God theory, not its possible content. But we do not have to go into detail to recall that there is no single universally accepted account of the commands of God: that despite some overlaps, the different world-religions are by no means in agreement over what God in fact commands—the loving of one's neighbour, the scrupulous following of ritual observances, and so on. There are conflicts here, in other words, conflicts that surely cannot be resolved by a *further* appeal to divine commands.

Let us look back over this section. We have been asking how far we can show that underlying the enormous multiplicity of our duties, rights and ideals there is some single supreme principle of morality that gives all these their *raison d'être* and makes them intelligible. We could have investigated many other alleged 'supreme principles', e.g. 'All our duties and all our ideals are concerned with the furthering of evolutionary advance', or 'The object of the moral life is "self-realisation"'. The theories that we chose to consider keep recurring in the history of thought, and certainly feature in any study of moral philosophy which does not break altogether with tradition. But in all of them we found serious difficulties. Important areas of moral experience were not adequately coped with, the ideal commanded had only a spurious unity, or the 'ultimate authority' turned out not in fact to be ultimate.

It might look as if the way were open again to seeing morality as a quite chaotic miscellany of rules and ideals, lacking any intelligible structure. If so, we should be back to 'square one'. But that would be a misleading conclusion, for several reasons. The hedonistic utilitarian may succeed in replying effectively to his critics: as I took care to say, we have looked at only the first moves in a continuing debate. Alternatively, one of the other single-principle theories might conceivably succeed where utilitarianism failed. And thirdly even if all one-principle theories do fail (as I think they do), there may still remain important relationships to discover among the various ideals and duties—even though these cannot be deduced from any single principle. Some moral policies, for instance, conflict with each other and cannot harmoniously coexist in an integrated moral life. If candour and openness are highly valued in all personal dealings, the reward of intrigue and double-dealing cannot be simultaneously enjoyed. If a person adopts certain attitudes and roles that he judges of value, he may find that they also oust other capacities that he did not wish to lose. The cynical or ironical man may find his cynicism corroding what he wished to esteem and enjoy.

Thus although there turned out to be several components, it would not follow that they are disconnected atoms, having no intelligible relations with one another. To say that they cannot be *deduced* from a single component is not to deny them every sort of inter-relation: deducibility is only one out of many relationships in which they could stand. To endorse a particular moral ideal may be to choose a *complex*—a way of life in which the ideal is embedded, and which excludes other human possibilities. Moreover, to see what hangs together with what, what excludes what, and what *leads* to what, is an investigation that the moralist does not undertake alone. He must tackle it in collaboration with the psychologist and the sociologist, with the serious novelist and the playwright.

Freedom and Responsibility

Moral philosophy, we have noted, is concerned not only with the sort of problems we have just been exploring. It is also interested in questions of a different sort. Under what conditions, it asks, is a human being properly to be held morally responsible? To that question the most obvious and important answer is: 'A man is responsible only if he acts *freely*.' The answer is obvious enough: but it is not nearly so obvious what exactly we mean here by 'freely', what we mean when we say we have 'free-will', or whether we have such a thing.

Perhaps the best way of being introduced to the free-will problem is not through the exposition of one possible theory of freedom, but through the simultaneous deploying of several approaches—in dialogue with one another. This is the plan to be followed in the remainder of the chapter.

If the reader wishes, he can begin the dialogue now (p. 116), ignoring the intervening pages. I preface the dialogue, however, with a brief statement of its 'argument' in case the detail of the conversation itself should make it difficult, on a first reading, to discern its principal themes.

. . . .

Two philosophers, Black and Green, agree that the free-will problem is serious and complex, though they look in different directions for a possible solution to it. White overhears their dispute, and at first doubts very much whether such heavy weather need be made of it. For him, there are familiar, commonsensical tests for freedom and its absence. A person is free, so long as he is not pushed around or compelled to act against his will. There is no more to it than that.

Black denies this. To him, there is no fundamental difference between external compulsions of a gross and obvious sort, and the determining of our actions in very complicated, unseen ways, by what goes on in our central nervous systems, ductless glands and so on. In other words, Black argues that we should have no real freedom, if all our actions were the result of prior causes; and the causes would not have to be interventions from without. We cannot see an act as properly *our own* and feel responsible for it, if it is really a complex product of our heredity and environment—if, given these factors, the act could not have happened differently.

But what is the alternative? Is a free act to be an act that has *no causes at all*? White has been a little disturbed by Black's reasoning, and he tries out this new possibility: could free acts be acts that are uncaused, spontaneous new starts?

Green sees this as a retrograde step. Acts that have no causes would be acts that happen 'out of the blue', anomalous events for which nobody could hold himself responsible. If the continuity of cause-and-effect relations is broken in this way, we *lose* responsibility rather than *gain* it—for we break also the thread of continuity between the agent's past behaviour and his present act. To defend himself against this, Black has to make a distinction between different *types* of continuity. Cause-and-effect relations might suffer interruption (he argues) without there being a break in continuity of *purpose* and *intention*. So we could make room for genuinely free acts without having to see them as mere anomalies.

This, however, raises enormous new issues. How exactly are we to relate our talk about causes to our talk about purposes, intentions, choices and reasons for choices? White originally suggested that, so long as I choose to do what I in fact do, then I act freely without there being any interruptions of cause-and-effect relationships. Now he is much less sure. If a choice itself is causally determined, are choices what we normally think them to be? Or have they turned out to be illusory? And what happens when we make an effort to do our duty, against the grain of inclinations and traits of character? If our 'tryings' also are causally determined, can we properly be praised for trying hard, or blamed for not trying hard enough?

This raises the question: What is the *point* of blamings and praisings? If, for instance, blaming is primarily a way of causally modifying someone's behaviour, there would still seem to be a place for it even if all actions were causally determined.

But that account of blaming is too simple. We blame or praise *moral agents*: and to be a moral agent is to be capable of self-understanding, insight and reasoning. Can there be complete causal determinism, and there yet remain a place for these—for rationality, that is? Black, of course, denies this. To him, there is a profound distinction between being determined by causal conditions to utter a sentence, 'S', and being convinced on good rational grounds that 'S' is true.

Green, on the contrary, sees no clash, no necessary opposition, between causal determination and the possibility of reasoning and rational insight. The two may coexist. With some help from the perplexed and uncertain White, the rest of the dialogue explores this problem.

. . . .

White: I cannot really see why the free-will problem need worry anyone for long. Surely a person is free when he can do what he wants to do, what he chooses to do; when nothing stands in his way. Such a man is responsible for what he does.

Black: You mean: the only thing that can take my freedom away is some external constraint, some compulsion—like being locked in a cell or being forced to press a trigger because a stronger hand is over my hand?

White: That's it. If someone is gripping your hand, you aren't responsible for firing the gun. You don't really *act* at all.

Green: True enough. Constraints and compulsions like these certainly don't go with freedom. But they are not the only kind that we need to think about. As well as those external compulsions there are also various kinds of internal compulsion, internal constraint. You would need to add these to your list, I think. A mentally ill person may be unable to prevent himself acting in some fashion—stealing perhaps, or harming someone who, he knows, wishes him well. *He* is not free, is he?

White: Well, we can add internal compulsions to the external ones. I don't object. It is the same with being *unable* to act: there isn't just the prison cell, but there is also the paralysis that may take away one's ability to act just as effectively. That can be due to some malfunctioning in the brain.

All this seems straightforward enough to me. Where are these philosophical *cruces*?

Black: They aren't far away. There are cases where a brain surgeon can operate and correct a malfunction, where drugs or electric-shock therapy help mental illness, where tiny changes in the working of a ductless gland can make an astonishing difference to a personality. Now in all these cases the person's behaviour may once again become acceptable to himself and to society. But, acceptable though it be, his behaviour and his general personality are still very intimately related to the working of these complex mechanisms with which the therapists have been tinkering—his central nervous system, his glands and so on. The fact that these manipulations are possible makes this dramatically obvious. Now many people, rightly or wrongly, go on to argue like this. 'Normal health,' they will say, 'and mental or physical illnesses are different from each other in numerous ways; but it looks as if they do not differ in one respect, that there are causal conditions, causal determinations, for *everything* a human being does, feels, or thinks.' And so, they ask with some bewilderment: 'what happens to freedom?'

That's only one way into the problem; there are many others.

White: Surely it still remains true that the person who is a victim of constraints (external or internal) or is prevented from acting (by locked doors or by paralysis) cannot do what he wants to do, chooses to do; and the person who is not a victim of any of these *can* do what he wants to do. Isn't this enough to save freedom? There is no *illusion* in this distinction. Or am I missing the point?

Green: No, I think you are absolutely right. We have to resist this switching over from talk about compulsions that certainly do take away freedom, to talk about causes that *don't* in fact take it away. I think that there may well be a causal explanation for all behaviour, that all of it may have causes, and yet freedom is not an illusion: we are responsible when we aren't constrained. But don't think that this is obvious or easy to demonstrate.

Black: Yes, it is very hard to demonstrate; but that's because it is quite false. I'll start again on a different tack. I'll try to show that our acts cannot be free and at the same time be the effects of prior causes.

Let us suppose that all happenings do have causes; that in theory we could show how all the events happening at the present moment (call it 'time *t*' for short) are the result of what happened the moment before. (We'll call the moment before 'time $t-1$'.) Now it follows that if we wanted to change anything that is happening at time *t*—to make it turn out differently—we'd have to change the state of affairs at $t-1$. But we cannot do that, since $t-1$ is in the past, and nothing can alter what's in the past. Finally, suppose one of the events occurring at time *t* is an action of mine. It too must be the result of what happened at $t-1$. That means I have no power to make it turn out differently from how it does turn out, no real freedom; since to alter the act I should again need to alter its antecedents at $t-1$, and that moment is inaccessibly past. (It's no use, of course, saying, 'I missed my chance: I should have intervened back at $t-1$.' For what happened *then* depended entirely on the state of affairs at $t-2$, and so on.) Immanuel Kant used this argument in his *Critique of Practical Reason*: '. . . as time past is no longer in my power, . . . every action that I perform must be the necessary result of certain determining grounds *which are not in my power*: that is, at the moment in which I am acting, I am never free.' (In fact, Kant himself argued that we *are* free, nevertheless; but I don't mean to go into the details of his positive view.) What I am arguing now is this—that you cannot believe both that all our actions are entirely determined by causes prior in time, *and* that we have freedom.

White: But we *do* know we are free. I have a good deal more assurance in saying that than I have in any intricate precarious argument.

Black: Maybe you have assurance. A flat-earth believer may have plenty assurance too. The question is whether your assurance is well-grounded. Don't you see that if what a person does is wholly determined by past events, even *immediately* past ones, and those by earlier events and so on, that it's nonsense to call that person responsible for his act? The act can't be seen as *his* any more, but only as the inescapable product of what's come before. It's not spontaneous; it's not free. On this account, it is determined partly by the agent's heredity, his given constitution and capacities. (He had no share in deciding what these would be.) And for the rest, it is determined by his environment, as that has acted upon and has interacted with those hereditary factors. What room does that account leave for freedom?

White: I see the problem. . . . Yet, suppose, just for the sake of argument, that I were convinced by what Black has been saying, I don't think I'd have to deny that there is any freedom. How should I argue? . . . I'd point out that we have not at all proved that every event does have a cause; and I don't see how that *could* be proved anyway, since we can't possibly check on *all* events to see if they have causes or not. Now then (I'd go on), when we act *freely* . . .

Green: Careful! This line of argument leads straight to the quicksands.

Black: Leave him alone: there's nothing so firm about the ground *you* want to stand on.

White: Let me try this out. . . . In acting freely, we assess all the factors that have made our situation what it is and have made our own character what it is. Then, I suppose, we stand back and *choose* how to act, aware of all the inclinations and proddings, but *determined*—caused to act—by none of them.

Green: Maybe that's how it feels when we reflect and choose: but you'd be wrong in imagining these acts have to be un-caused. Your original view was the sounder one.

White: All the same, it does seem reasonable enough to say that an act *may* have no cause—for all we know.

Green: Yes, but that is quite beside the point. Do you remember how Black said a minute ago that if all our behaviour is causally determined by earlier events and those events by still earlier events, then we'd no longer be able to call any events *our own actions*—to identify ourselves with them? I want to say: precisely the same objection can be made to speculations about acts that have no causes.

White: What do you mean? If one said that some acts are not fully determined, that would be to deny their being merely the working out of *other* events, of heredity and environment.

Black: Yes, you would be trying to make it possible for an act to be spontaneous, a new intervention. . . .

Green: But making it un-caused cannot do any of these things. If what I do has really no cause—no cause at all—how can I possibly hold myself responsible for it? Such an act is *nobody*'s act: it happens out of the blue. To say it has no causal explanation is to say 'inexplicable', 'anomalous', or 'random'—and to say it about the act which a person most of all wants to identify himself with and accept as his own. How can he, once he has thought through what it means to have no cause?

White: Black, it was you who insisted that we cannot be free if every event has a cause. How do you escape this dilemma?—or *can* it be escaped?

Black: Yes; Green has not said the last word. The problem is, how I can claim that an act is uncaused, and yet think of it as my *own* act? Well, causal connexions are not the only kind of connexions. Suppose you ask me why I did a particular action. I tell you a story, not about this causing that, which then causes the next thing, but about my plans or intentions, i.e. about the rational *point* of the action, how it fits my purposes, or what *reasons* there were for doing this rather than something else. So long as I can tell such a story, my action is not random or anomalous.

Green: That does not convince me. It still leaves a discontinuity, a gap between the agent as a person with a history and determinate character, a continuous complex of processes in time—on the one hand—and the particular 'causeless' act he is said to perform—on the other hand. It's *fortunate* if the act does fit in with an agent's purposes and plans: but if we seriously claim that nothing whatever caused it, can this fitting in be more than a lucky chance?

Look here: although White had no idea how complicated this problem is, he started on absolutely the right tack. 'A person is free,' he said, 'when he can do what he wants to do, what he chooses to do . . .' So long as you have choice, and your action flows from your choice, then you have freedom. It is meaningful to speak of being freed from constraints and compulsions that take away the power of choice or force you to do what you have chosen not to do. But it isn't meaningful in the least to speak of being free from causal continuity: that way lies *ir*responsibility.

White: Yes, that was my view at the outset: but now you have made me worried. It certainly sounded safe enough—'If I do what I choose to do, I can't fail to be free. . . .'

Green: That is the very *meaning* of 'free' in this context. If you are trying to prove in court that *A* was responsible for injuring B, you don't try to show that *A*'s acts had no causes. Much help that would be! You try to show that *A meant* to injure *B*, decided, chose to injure him: and that is enough.

White: Yet, what worries me is this. It's about the 'choosing' itself—we shall have to say that the choosing is causally determined, that, things being as they were, it could not have failed to happen. So I now find myself strongly tempted to say that such a choosing is only an illusion of choice, a fixed wheel in a set of gears, merely passing on the impetus from event before to event after. And that is not how I normally think of choice.

Black: Quite so: you think of it more as a gear lever, intervening to make *changes* in the speed and direction of travel. . . . ?

Green: We shan't really advance this discussion by working out picturesque analogies!

White: At least it points up my sense of dissatisfaction. You see, with 'wanting' something equally odd happens. Doing what I want to do would be still a *satisfactory* state of affairs: but on this view, if my wantings at any moment are the effects of a complex set of causal factors, can I think of this state of affairs as an exercise of *freedom*—any more than with a lowly organism whose instinct leads it to its proper food?

Green: All right. You are puzzled: and I don't deny that there is plenty here to be puzzled about. But if you argue that an act of choice somehow becomes illusory if it is causally determined, then you should be able to tell me what would make it real, *non*-illusory?

White: I don't know: it would have to be in some way *voluntary*. But what 'voluntary' could mean here, I'm not at all sure. . . . In at least some contexts 'voluntary' itself means 'chosen'.

Green: There's no help in that direction. You would be saying this: that an act is free only if it is chosen, and the choice (in order to be a real, free choice) must itself be chosen. . . . In this way we should have started upon an endless series of choices, each choice needing a previous choice to give it its spontaneity. But one cannot go through an infinite series of choices before acting. What you have here is a *reductio ad absurdum*, a refutation, of that account of choice and freedom. What makes a choice a real choice, spontaneous and free, *cannot* be the fact that it is itself chosen. That, of course, supports my case: so long as there is no compulsion or constraint, no inner or outer pushings and pullings, then there is no threat to freedom; choices can be taken at their face value. They are *effective*: what is done is what is chosen. Could you ask for more than that?

Black: I'm sorry; but that won't rescue the situation. You say, 'so long as there are no inner or outer pushings and pullings . . .', but I argued with some care that to meet *this* condition involves denying that there is any causal determining of your will when you act freely. Sometimes causal determination is obvious and visible, as with external compulsions: sometimes it is internal and still evident enough, as in mental disturbances. But the 'pushings and pullings', the 'causal chains', as we often call them, don't have to be evident or visible in order to be *there* and to be operating. I cannot accept the distinction you make so glibly between constraints and causes.

Green: Perhaps that is because you are working once again with misleading analogies instead of hard argument. People take a few mechanical examples—an engine pulling coaches, a billiard-ball that taps other balls . . . and without any good reason they take these cases as revealing the essence of cause-and-effect relations. Event drags along event, although the couplings may be invisible. But what do we *really* experience? Events of one kind regularly following events of some other kind: a regular sequence, and that is all. The egg that's boiled for ten minutes is, regularly, hard. The taking of alcohol by a driver is regularly followed by impaired driving skill. Smoking and lung-cancer are well-correlated.

Of course we don't just passively watch what happens in the world, what follows what. As often as we can, we *intervene* in the world—change certain of the conditions, and see if the 'effect' occurs or fails to occur: we *make* the suspected cause occur, and see if the effect follows. And so on—with great complexity—in the experimental sciences. But we never see the 'cause' causing, we never see the mythical coupling, the causal chains: all we see is a regular pattern of event following event. *What* event follows what, only experience tells us. [Compare Hume's criticism of necessary connexion, p. 37. Green here relies on Hume's associated account of causation.]

So with human beings. To say that our acts are 'caused' is no more than to say that they too are explicable in terms of such patterns of regular sequence. In any case, *without* such regularities, we could never know or understand a human being, never grasp his character. There would be no continuity or consistency to him: we could never count on him acting one way rather than another. That does not make him a slave in causal chains.

Black: I could take you up on a number of points in all that. Your account of causality, for instance—by no means everyone would accept it. But I'll take a different topic. I don't want to deny that causality applies to a great part of our lives as persons, that we have characters, dispositions, regular ways of behaving. I want to deny only that this can be the whole story. To be free, I must sometimes be able to rise *above* my character as so far formed, to modify and reshape that character in various ways. Crucially, I must be able to 'rise to duty' (as some philosophers have put it), even when my character and inclinations prompt me strongly to neglect my duty instead.

White: That is true in one way. We do speak of taking ourselves in hand, of resisting inclinations, being dissatisfied with our habits and dispositions. But at the same time there is something very odd about the use you want to make of this. Surely you could equally well say that the conscientious side of my character is at war with the selfish and complacent sides of my character: that in rising to my duty I'm revealing the dominance of that conscientious side—not somehow escaping from my character altogether. It is only if you *do* put it in that way that you seem forced into a theory of uncaused acts or acts of will, in order to safeguard freedom.

Black: So whether or not I rise to my duty entirely depends on which disposition or strand in my character happens to be the strongest at the relevant moment. On that basis, it could not be fair ever to blame me for having failed to do some particular duty. If I fail to do it, that is because doing it was not in my power at that time. The conscientious side was not the dominant side, and that's that.

In this picture I simply do not recognise the life of freedom —moral freedom—at all.

Green: Perhaps that is because we haven't said anything specifically about *trying,* trying to do one's duty, trying to overcome inclinations to the contrary.

Black: Trying is a vital notion here, I agree. But I should be surprised if anything helpful could be said about trying —on *your* theory.

Green: My view can accommodate trying as well as it can accommodate choosing and deciding. Whether trying occurs or not is usually a crucial factor for attributing blame and praise for actions. On my account, of course, there are causal factors behind the trying, as there are behind every other set of events. But that makes no difference to the importance, the moral relevance, of the trying. A mentally normal person who *doesn't* try to resist an inclination, say, to be cruel, is morally blameworthy. That's one of our *criteria* for blameworthiness.

Black: It usually is, but it cannot be, on *your* theory. How can it be fair to blame a person, if he is causally determined not to try to resist the inclination; if the causal conditions are not such as to result in his trying? Or again: suppose he does try a little, or tries desperately hard, the degree to which he tries is exactly the degree to which the causal factors in him and his environment make trying possible and necessary. So once more there is no room left for blame or for praise either.

White: I see the difficulty: but I think Black is exaggerating it. There is *some* room left for blame and praise. If you blame someone or punish him, you make your disapproval known to him, you bring pressure upon him to act differently in future. You are changing the causal circumstances in which he is going to act next time. So with praising and rewarding. These are new causal factors, and may help to reinforce the tendency he has to act in the approved manner.

Black: That gives a kind of sense to blame and praise, I grant you. But it is not the sense they have in our ordinary moral thinking; and it isn't a humanly tolerable sense. On your view, praising and blaming become mere ways of *manipulating* people, however benignly. People are seen really as *things*, machines to be adjusted, overhauled, serviced and 'tuned'.

Green: It is easy to be rhetorical about it. The difficult thing is to say exactly what is missing from that account, if anything is missing. Where blame and punishment are concerned, it certainly fits in well with enlightened theories of deterring and reforming offenders, rather than being merely retributive. . . .

Black: Let me put it this way. Would you call it 'enlightened' to see punishment as 'conditioning' an offender not to repeat his offence?

Green: You mean, like conditioning a rat to take a certain route in an experimenter's maze: giving him a shock when he takes any other route?

Black: That's the sort of thing.

Green: No, there is an all-important difference. We hope the offender will have *insight* into what is wrong with his conduct: that he'll understand the point of his punishment. Rewarding and praising also presuppose insight and rationality.

White: Can we not say, more generally still, that to be a moral agent means first of all to be a *rational* being? To deliberate morally means to weigh up reasons for acting in this way or that way, to see what's relevant and irrelevant to your choice.

Black: I entirely agree. The moral life is possible only if reasoning is possible, if action can be chosen *in accordance with* the reasons pro and con—all other influence being irrelevant and 'alien'.

White: Ah, I know what you're going to say. It's something of a refrain. 'You cannot have causal determinism and rationality together.' If that is it, can you prove it?

Black: I think I can.

Suppose causal determinism is true: what I do, say, think or feel is the result of sets of prior events, events in my body, my nervous system, my cortex. My sense of conviction that a particular argument is valid, that this is a good reason for that, will be due no less to the operation of such causes. If the causes produce that effect (the sense of conviction), *when and only when* the reasoning is good reasoning, then everything is in order. But what possible grounds could we have for believing that it is so? There could exist no conceivable way of checking. Causes, as mere events, cannot be appraised as rational or irrational: they just occur. My sense of assurance about an argument would tell me that certain events were occurring in my brain—those events needed to produce that sense of assurance! But I could not rely on it telling me anything beyond that. When I move from step to step in an argument, each move I make is causally determined. But what I need is a quite *different* necessitation: not the working of alien causes, but the necessitation of logic alone; not being forced by causal factors, but being convinced on good grounds.

Green: No; here you are really in a confusion. You are saying that if the steps of our reasoning are causally determined, we can't trust our reasoning to be valid: causal determination may prompt us to write or utter a 'conclusion' that is no conclusion in logic, that doesn't follow. So that there is no rationality, if determination is true.

But think a moment. Does it matter in the least whether we can give a causal account of a piece of reasoning, so long as that reasoning conforms to the laws of logic, the canons of good argument? And of course we do have such canons. Suppose I work out a mathematical problem on paper. You point at a particular line of the working, and say, 'Why did you put that there?' I could give you two different sorts of answer: 'Because that's how I was taught it at school; that's the drill'—a causal and autobiographical story. Or I might say, 'Because this line *follows* from the line above'—a story in terms of *reasons*. The two stories are (crucially) *compatible* stories: they don't fight or interfere with each other. They can both be true. The first interprets the question as a request for causal explanation; the other as a request for a rational justification: both can be had. And *because* both can be had, determinism doesn't rule out rationality.

White: I should like to believe you are right. But I'm uneasy at one point.

Black: You have every reason to be. Go on.

White: I agree that we have these two ways of speaking about an argument, the causal way and the rational or logical way. But *is* it all right to say, 'No matter about causality, provided we can assess the argument logically'?

What is in question is just our ability to *do* that, our wanting to be sure that when we *suppose* we are doing it (with a sense of conviction that we have proved validity or invalidity), we are *really* doing it, that we aren't being determined by essentially non-rational causal factors to imagine we are doing what we aren't doing.

Black: Thank you: that is my point. You have undermined your own position very thoroughly in making it.

White: Well . . . what I am saying is all very tentative. For instance, I'm not sure that I can make any better sense of reasoning going on *without* any causal determination—our old problem again.

Green: Yes indeed: several things have been said already in our discussion that apply here also. All along I have argued that in order to be morally free, you don't have to be free from *causality* (that is absurd), but free from certain specific constraints, compulsions. In the absence of these you are free, in the vital sense that nothing prevents your deliberating what to do and doing what you decide to do. To ask for more is to ask the inconceivable. So too—I want to say—with reason and reasoning. How do you tell if a person's action is reasonable, if his policy is rational? Among other things, we should look for an essential *flexibility* that goes with discriminating power. For example, the rational man takes precautions against assault from another person only when that person has given signs of hostility and violence. The irrationally 'persecuted' man suspects everyone indiscriminately and inflexibly. The man whose political allegiance is rational will think again and leave his party, if its policy changes in morally important ways. The party member who was *indoctrinated* into allegiance, whose allegiance is irrational, will be immune to such reappraisals.

Now there are the closest ties between rationality and freedom. I think we are all agreed about that. To say that a man has freely chosen some line of conduct, is to say he hasn't been cajoled, threatened, brainwashed into accepting it. He has been able to reflect on the alternatives, and decide among them according to the reasons pro and con. The more clearly he is aware of the alternatives and their consequences, the less is he working in the dark and the greater is his freedom.

My main point is this. The *measure* of that freedom is the measure of those factors I've been listing: Was there indoctrination? Were there threats? How fully could the agent grasp the alternatives? Would his choice have varied as the *situation* varied?—that is to say, was it flexible or inflexible behaviour? These and the like questions are the tests for rationality and freedom in action.

White: Before you go further. You are speaking about the 'measure' of freedom, about a greater and a less. You imply that there are *degrees* of freedom; that it is not simply *either-or*—free or not free. If that is what you mean, it seems reasonable enough to me; but it surely clashes with other things that have been said in our discussion.

Green: I certainly do want to say that freedom has degrees.

White: But think about the attempt to interpret free acts as 'uncaused'. Whether an event is or isn't caused—that must be an either-or matter. It cannot be a matter of degree. So, if there are degrees of freedom . . .

Green: . . . we have further good reasons for rejecting that account. Certainly we have.

But I had not quite finished what I was saying about the tests for rationality and freedom. In fact, the conclusion I was drawing is the same conclusion White has drawn, though I was going to put it differently. The tests for rationality and freedom are familiar enough tests, and they are multiple tests. Moreover, none of them is a test for the presence or absence of causes!

You can see all this most clearly if you consider freedom in relation to self-knowledge. The relation between them is obviously a close one. For instance, a man driven by ill-understood, irrational passions is unfree, *passive* (etymologically, 'passion' is something *'suffered'*). The free man is free to the degree that he understands, and through understanding dominates, his passions. Once more, these discriminations are real and relevant, and nothing stops the determinist from recognising them.

Black: He can recognise these distinctions, I don't deny. But they are superficial and unimportant. The crux is this. If a man *does* dominate his passions, he could not have done otherwise—on the determinist view. If he *fails* to dominate them, again he could not have done otherwise. If it's no longer (say) unconscious feelings of guilt that drive a man to act, then the causes of his action have changed—and have become more complex—but they haven't ceased to *determine* what he does.

Now don't tell me that a man can act otherwise, if he chooses so to act. We have been through all that: if his choice itself is determined, your appeal to choice does not help to give freedom to his action.

So: accept causal determinism, and out goes freedom, out goes rationality.

White: But we three have been arguing—more or less rationally. A *determinist* argues when he sets out the case for determinism. You would refute yourself if you used reasoning to prove that reasoning cannot be replied upon. It follows from that . . .

Green: It follows that a determinist has to show that causal determination does *not* rule out rationality; and that is one of the things I've been labouring to show.

Black: Not at all. What follows is this: since the determinist theory does undermine rationality, we must reject that theory, if we are going to save both rationality and the freedom that is tied up with it. However difficult it is to understand the libertarian view, we implicitly adopt it every time we reason, deliberate, or make a choice.

White: As far as I am concerned, you have both succeeded in one way and both failed in another. In fact, it's your success that leads to your failure. I have had to grant that what I said at the start was a good deal too simple; and I cannot any more see a short-cut to an answer. There you win.

But, on the other hand, none of your longer and more complex accounts has really convinced me—as yet. I need much clearer ideas of causality and of human action, a clearer idea about what one needs to be free from in order to be morally responsible. I am not at all sure now whether causal explanations do or do not undermine rational explanations. . . .

Black: Cheer yourself up by putting the same point in a positive way. The short statement of a philosophical problem is always a deceptive statement: 'Is the will free?', 'Is the soul immortal?' If you manage to identify the complex cluster of questions to which the statement vaguely points, then you have begun to advance some way towards a reliable answer. *Fail* to do that, and the problems will remain quite intractable.

5
Social and Political Philosophy

H. B. Acton

Scope of the Subject

A student who examines the syllabuses and the recommended books for degrees in history, in politics and in philosophy in a typical British University, will notice that these subjects appear to have a common course which in the history syllabus is often called Political Theory, in the politics syllabus may have the same title or even be called Political Ideologies, and in the philosophy course is called Political Philosophy. The title is sometimes Social Philosophy or even Social and Political Philosophy. This nomenclature is discussed on p. 138 below. What makes it appear a common course is that such topics as sovereignty, freedom, natural rights and democracy, and such books as Aristotle's *Politics,* Rousseau's *Social Contract* and J. S. Mill's *On Liberty* are listed for discussion in all of them. In some universities one teacher takes the same course for three different degree subjects. In others, each department has its own course taught by one of its own teachers.

Let us now briefly consider what is being chiefly aimed at in the courses intended for students of history and for students of politics. The Political Theory studied by a student of history is largely concerned with political ideas which are thought to have had a major influence upon the events of history or to have given expression to the outlook and aspirations of their times. Thus, Rousseau's *Social Con-*

tract was repeatedly referred to by leaders of the French Revolution, and in it is set out the then revolutionary view that the people ought to be sovereign and governments ought to carry out their will. In studying this book, therefore, historians may hope to improve their understanding of an important crisis in European history and to get some idea of how the democratic standpoint was defended in the eighteenth century.

The student of politics will not ignore these things, but he will be more concerned with the specific forms of government which Rousseau recommended. He will notice, for example, that Rousseau favoured direct democracy, that is, rule by the whole people voting its laws directly, and thought little of representative democracy, that is, rule by the people through elected representatives who vote the laws on behalf of the electors. The British people, Rousseau said, were only free once in seven years—at that time Parliament was elected for seven years, not for five as at present—and were not free in between as they could not vote on the matters that Parliament was discussing and deciding but had to accept their representatives' decisions. The student of politics pays particular attention to the different sorts of political constitution and modes of government. Hence he reads Rousseau's *Social Contract* for the light it throws on types of democratic rule and on the reasons put forward in favour of them.

We may see a similar difference of emphasis between the historian's interest in John Stuart Mill's *On Liberty* and that of the student of politics. The historian sees Mill as anxious for the reform or repeal of the Blasphemy Laws and as an opponent of much of the temperance legislation that was being proposed and introduced in the United States and Great Britain at the time he was writing the book. Thus the historian looks at *On Liberty* in the context of mid-nineteenth-century politics where it was untypical and not very influential.

The student of politics is particularly concerned with a rather different aspect of the book. Mill, like his father and Bentham before him, had been a supporter of democracy, but in *On Liberty* he expressed his fear that democratic rule would stifle originality and individuality. His political object was to indicate ways in which these things could be preserved in a democratic society where most people were indifferent or even hostile to them. Thus the student of politics is particularly concerned with Mill's opposition to censorship and his view that legal and social prohibitions can only be justifiably imposed against conduct which causes definite harm or injury to other people, but not against conduct that harms only the doer of it himself.

Now the student of philosophy (whom from now onwards we shall call the philosopher) must learn something about the historical context and must understand how the various types of institution such as kingship, parliaments, courts of law and police differ from and are related to one another. If he were ignorant of history and of the basic terminology of politics he would not be equipped for the study of political philosophy. Granted that he has acquired this fundamental knowledge, however, the philosopher has to pursue some problems much further than is necessary for the historian or the student of politics.

An example may be taken from Rousseau's *Social Contract*. It was Rousseau's view that when individuals formed a society they formed a body with a *general will*. Members of a society with a general will had *particular wills* of their own. As members or citizens of the society, they participated in its general will, and as law-breakers or recalcitrants they pursued their own *particular interests* and in so doing went against the general will in which they had participated. Rousseau calls the society with a general will 'a moral and collective body', and says that it has 'its unity, its common self, its life'. He says, too, that the man who, in a state with a general will, accepts the benefits it brings him but neglects his duties to it, really 'regards the moral person which constitutes the state as a thing of reason, because it is not a man'. In being punished, Rousseau concludes, such a man 'will be forced to be free'.

Now the philosopher will have a number of things to ask about this view. Rousseau appears to think that, besides the particular wills of individual men, there is the will of 'the moral and collective body', the will of 'the moral person'. Is he only speaking metaphorically? No, his own words go against this interpretation, for it is the selfish man, Rousseau says, who regards the moral person as a 'thing of reason', that is, as a mere fiction, and Rousseau implies that the selfish man is wrong about this. Are there, then, non-fictitious moral persons with general wills and general interests as well as particular persons with particular wills and particular interests? Do the individuals form such a moral person when they form a society? Is an individual man whose particular will is constrained by the general will of the society being forced to be free? Or is freedom, on the contrary, something that cannot be forced but must be spontaneous? These are some of the questions which the political philosopher will wish to pursue. Rousseau himself did not take them very far, but his words influenced not only such politicians as Robespierre, but also such philosophers as Hegel and his English follower Bernard Bosanquet. In philosophy the word 'Ontology' means the theory of what there is. Thus Rousseau's *Social Contract* raises a question of ontology, the question, whether states (and other communities) are real existences, or whether they are nothing but the way in which individual men (who do really exist) are related to one another and act together. It also raises a question about the connexion of our concepts, viz. whether being free necessarily entails not being coerced, or whether being free and being coerced are compatible with one another.

Let us now look at Mill's *On Liberty* to see how it appears as a contribution to political philosophy. Mill, unlike Rousseau, was a philosopher of wide scope. Mill's *Principles of Logic* has been widely read and discussed ever since its appearance, and his little book *Utilitarianism* has been thoroughly discussed as well. Mill regarded himself as upholding the philosophy of experience, as he called it, or Empiricism, as we call it today (see pp. 42 ff). The political philosopher, therefore, considers *On Liberty* as part of what was intended to be a comprehensive and consistent philosophical outlook. He will ask whether the view expressed in it that scope should be allowed for individuality, in the sense of freedom to follow one's own ideals and interests, is compatible with the view expressed in *Utilitarianism* that the aim of our actions should be the happiness of all. Again, in *On Liberty* Mill argues that whoever claims to suppress wrong opinions assumes his own infallibility. The political philosopher is, of course, concerned with the truth or falsity of this rather widespread view, but will be more inclined than the historian or student of politics to consider what infallibility is or could be and whether someone who says he knows something for certain is in fact claiming to be infallible in any way.

In our first paragraph, we mentioned that not only were there certain authors whose books were studied in courses intended for historians, for students of politics and for philosophers, but also that there are certain common topics, of which we mentioned sovereignty, freedom, natural rights and democracy. To take sovereignty as one example, the student of history is particularly concerned to ascertain when the notion of sovereignty came to be defined and to be regarded as important. He may remark that in mediaeval society the king, although the supreme political authority, was not regarded as the sole source of law as he came to be in the sixteenth and seventeenth centuries. The student of politics raises the question whether there is in fact a sovereign authority in every government and he may point out the difficulty of finding one in such a constitution as that of the United States, in which the President, although the chief executive and commander-in-chief, may have his legislation thrown out by Congress or interpreted by the Supreme Court in ways he does not like. The political philosopher needs to know about such things, but he will be particularly concerned with such questions as whether laws presuppose a single supreme law-making and law-enforcing authority and, more generally, whether authority is conceivable apart from power and coercion.

We are now in a position to make some general comments on the nature and scope of political philosophy. It is concerned with society and government, not primarily in order to trace its history or to describe and explain its institutions, but in order to gain a philosophical understanding of it. Hence the political philosopher explores the ontology of society, that is, the nature of states and other social groups in comparison with that of individual men. He also examines how the metaphysical, epistemological and ethical theories of philosophers and of types of philosophy are connected with the views about human society put forward by them. Plato, Aristotle, St. Thomas Aquinas, Hobbes, Spinoza, Locke, Kant, Hegel and Mill all expounded views about the social order which they held to be logically connected with their general philosophical positions. Were they right in thinking there was this connexion? Is there, for example, some logical connexion between empiricism and liberalism as Mill and others have suggested? Does Plato's rationalist view of knowledge, that is, his view that knowledge, as distinct from opinion, is independent of sense-experience, entail or support the sort of authoritarian political ideal which he put forward in the *Republic*? Spinoza too, had a rationalist view of knowledge, but this did not lead him to advocate authoritarian rule. Either, then, Spinoza was inconsistent, or else there is nothing in rationalist epistemology that necessitates the superiority of rule by an intellectual aristocracy.

It is not only in the writings of philosophers, however, that reasons are given for preferring one sort of society or government to others. For example, the politician Edmund Burke, in criticising the French Revolution of 1789, criticised radicalism in general and gave reasons in favour of social and political conservatism. The political philosopher who examines Burke's writings today endeavours to disentangle the arguments from the rhetoric in which they are clothed. He may also confront them with the radical criticisms of Burke put forward by Thomas Paine. Are there any general reasons for preferring the *status quo, any status quo*, to the prospects held out by reformers? On what grounds can it be said that all men have natural rights (or, as it is put today in the United Nations Declaration), human rights? What sorts of reasons are given for social and political equality, or for inequality and hierarchy? In considering these matters the political philosopher is trying to exhibit the logic of political argumentation. No doubt he will be able to expose fallacies—for example he may show that it is wrong to say that whoever tries to suppress an opinion assumes that he himself is infallible. But it is likely that he will exhibit the structure of various types of conflicting arguments without being able to show that one is incontestably superior to the other. But if refutation is seldom possible, understanding frequently is. In this respect the political philosopher is like the historian in being more detached from practical possibilities than the student of politics is. The historian wishes to understand how things came about, the political philosopher to understand the nature of the arguments and concepts used. The student of politics wants to understand too, but is also interested in considering how procedures might be improved or what new devices might be introduced. Thus he gets into such topics as the growing power of the executive or the functions of advisory boards. Even so, there is a great deal of common ground, and the political philosopher cannot afford to be ignorant either of the historical context of political concepts nor of the types of political institutions and modes of changing them. Nor should he forget that writers on politics sometimes have important things to say about what he regards as his main concern. The political philosopher who wants to understand the conception of a general will, for example, has much to learn from studies of the theory of voting which have been made by writers on politics and economics.

In some universities, courses are given in *social* philosophy rather than *political* philosophy, and very occasionally the course is called Social and Political Philosophy. It is generally intended that such courses should contain discussion of economic institutions, churches, the family, educational bodies, as well as of the state. The term 'politics' is derived from *polis*, which meant a city state in the writings of Plato and Aristotle, and hence there has been a strong tendency to regard politics as a study of the state and of government, and political philosophy as concerned with the philosophy of states and governments. In terms of this nomenclature, politics would be the theory of states and governments and sociology the theory of social institutions generally, and hence political philosophy would relate to politics, and social philosophy would be a wider subject relating to sociology. The important thing is that we understand the things being discussed—then differences of terminology will present few difficulties. In fact, Aristotle included under the heading of politics not only discussion of the state and government, but also as Plato had done, education as well. When philosophers talk of political philosophy they do not generally intend to exclude what does not belong to the state or government. They recognise the difference between society, the wider conception, and the state, a specific form of society alongside others. While, therefore, courses called social philosophy are obviously intended to deal with other things besides the philosophy of government, political philosophy, as generally understood, is usually meant to do the same. It would certainly be a truncated and misleading study if the only concepts and arguments considered in it were those concerning the state itself. (It should be noticed that 'government' is a wider conception than that of the state since schools, trades unions, churches have their governing bodies.)

At this stage it will be as well to illustrate the account we have so far given of the scope of political philosophy by indicating the main lines of argument and analysis on one or two central problems. Let us start with the differences between conservatism and radicalism. We shall not, of course, be concerned with the doctrines of political parties with those names, but with something more fundamental, which we shall now endeavour to clarify.

Conservatism and Radicalism

These are not systems of doctrine but important attitudes or points of view. The conservative tends to accept the social order as it is. He may favour improvements in matters of detail, in so far as they are practicable, but he rejects the idea of reforming society at its very roots. The radical, however, as the name implies (Latin *radix*, a root; radicalism is not always 'left-wing'), believes in reforming society from the roots upward. Tinkering with this or that particular evil, he believes, is a waste of time, since the particular evils must be symptomatic of something basically wrong. Plato gave expression to the radical attitude in the *Republic* when he said that trying to make detailed but isolated improvements in society was like trying to kill the Hydra by cutting off its heads one by one; as soon as some heads were cut off from this mythical beast, others sprang up elsewhere and the job of killing it was no further forward. The conservative, then, wants as little disturbance as possible, the radical is for movement, revolution, and progress.

It might be suggested, in the first place, that there are these two types of people with their contrasting *temperaments*, and that reasoning or argumentation is irrelevant to temperaments. We, however, have spoken of the conservative and radical *attitudes* or *points of view*, and we might equally well have used the word *'outlooks'*. Now attitudes are like temperaments in that we attribute them to individual human beings. But they are nevertheless unlike temperaments too, for temperaments are native dispositions, or dispositions acquired as a result of some accident or illness, which are extremely difficult to alter even if they are alterable at all. In ancient times human temperaments were classified into the sanguine, melancholic and choleric and so on, and no one supposes that they could be changed by argument. It may be said that men of melancholy temperament tend to adopt conservative attitudes, and men of sanguine temperament tend to adopt radical attitudes. If so, it is only a tendency, since, to take one example, Abraham Lincoln, a man of strongly marked melancholic temperament, certainly adopted some radical attitudes. Attitudes, however, are discussable and alterable. So and so, we say, changed his attitude towards the Common Market after reading such and such a book about it. Since attitudes, unlike temperaments, are discussable and alterable, they come into the sphere of rational argument. That is why attitudes are very much like points of view and outlooks, which are also amenable to rational exposition, explanation, vindication. When we speak, then, of conservative and radical attitudes, we are speaking of things which, like points of view and outlooks, can be considered in a rational manner by those who have them.. We may notice, in passing, that we have raised an interesting problem here, the problem of how to distinguish between the various states or frames of mind and personality that we say people have. Temperaments, we have suggested, are less rationally controllable than attitudes, and attitudes, we have suggested, can come under discussion in the way in which points of view or outlooks can.

What sort of attitude, then, is the conservative attitude? The conservative likes society as it is well enough not to want it upset or altered in any fundamental way. Burke said in his *Reflections on the Revolution in France* (1790), that the English supporters of the French Revolution argued about the social order 'as if the constitution of our country were to be always a subject rather of altercation than enjoyment'. Professor Michael Oakeshott in an essay entitled 'On being conservative' (*Rationalism in Politics*, 1962) says that central to the conservative 'disposition' (a word meaning, here, the same as what I called 'attitude') is 'a propensity to use and to enjoy what is available rather than to wish for or to look for something else'. He goes on to say that it involves preferring the familiar to the unknown, stability to rapid change. He argues that innovations seldom turn out as hoped and are less predictable the more extensive they are. He asserts that it is only when there is a stable background and change is gradual that people can preserve their identity. For when change is rapid and discontinuous, no one knows where he stands or even who he is. Oakeshott does not develop the argument in detail, but we may illustrate it by considering the difference between a child brought up in a stable family with parents who are constantly at hand to provide consistent support, and a child with no parents, handed from one minder to another, receiving different and inconsistent advice. The first is able to develop a personality and to think of *himself* as acting in the world and receiving things from it. The second does not know what he should do, and becomes a bundle of conflicting hopes and fears.

The radical, for his part, considers that the conservative attitude is both obtuse (in the last century radically-minded people called the Tory party 'the stupid party') and callous. To enjoy what is there without considering how it could be improved, says the radical, is refusing to apply the human reason to the human situation; and to enjoy and support a social order in which many people, perhaps the majority, suffer is to fail in human sympathy. The radical, finding that much is bad in human society, calls for its transformation in the light of rational principles and ideals. The radical appeals to the Rights of Man and to the principle of Equality of Opportunity, saying that social institutions should be altered and new ones devised in order that these principles should be realised. His idea is that society should be consciously and deliberately re-fashioned. It is only in the childhood of the human race that social arrangements can be accepted without discussion. Civilised men should re-create their society, should, indeed, re-create man himself. (Burke quotes a French revolutionary who had said that everything should be destroyed in order that everything could be changed—ideas, laws, things, words, men themselves.) Radicals, however, would say that Burke's word 'altercation' is an abusive way of describing rational argument. No rule. practice or institution, they maintain, should be withdrawn from rational discussion. Men are rational beings and they abjure their humanity if they allow their social arrangements to remain irrational, disordered and mysterious.

Now the conservative who undertakes to defend his attitude or point of view against the criticisms of radicals necessarily finds himself in an awkward position. For as we have seen, he is opposed to 'altercation' (rational argument) about the foundations of his society, and yet he himself engages in it when he presents or defends his point of view. We may call this the Paradox of Conservatism. The conservative endeavours to resolve this paradox by criticising the radical's view of what rational discussion is. That is, he defends his word 'altercation' on the ground that what the radical calls rational discussion is only rational in a degenerate or incomplete sense of the word. That there is a problem about what rational thinking really is, is apparent in the history of the theory of knowledge; but for our present purposes we need only note the distinction drawn by Pascal between 'l'esprit de géometrie' and 'l'esprit de finesse', that is between abstract reasoning of the mathematical type on the one hand, and reasoning based on long and deep experience and issuing in subtle intuitive judgements on the other. From Burke (indeed from Aristotle) onwards conservatives have denied that reasoning of the abstract mathematical type is relevant in social and political affairs. They say, furthermore, that this is the type of reasoning that radicals tend to make use of. 'These are the rights of man,' radicals say, 'grasped by the intellectual faculty in all men; so let us reconstruct society so as to conform to them. These rights are the same in Africa and Asia as in Europe and America, just as Pythagoras's Theorem is true in all these regions too.' On the contrary, says Burke, 'The science of constructing a commonwealth, or renovating it, or reforming it, is, like every other experimental science, not to be taught *a priori*.' Political activity requires tact, an appreciation of subtle gradations and distinctions, a sense of timing and of relevance. These are things that cannot be set out in definite rules and precepts. They are learned from doing and trying to do, as an art is learned.

The conservative, then, says that radicals have an inadequate conception of what reason is. Oakeshott has used the word 'rationalism' for this inadequate conception. There are at least two elements in its inadequacy. One of them is that in political activity the reasoning involved is quite different from the abstract reasoning of mathematics. The other is that the ideals and principles invoked by radicals are not, like principles of logic, common to all men and societies, but are elicited from or are 'abridgements' of (the word is Oakeshott's) the society within which they are formulated. Locke, for example, in his *Second Treatise of Civil Government*, may seem to be expounding certain universal principles of legitimate government, but in fact, according to the view we are expounding, he is presenting an abbreviated and abstracted version of English parliamentary government. Radicals, therefore, are never as radical as they wish to be, for they necessarily build their ideals with materials from their social inheritance.

The radical may object to this that if the radical can never be as radical as he sets out to be, then he is less formidable and less reprehensible than the conservative says he is. It is a strange way to attack radicalism, it may be said, to argue that it isn't possible anyway. It may also be pointed out that not all criticism is *radical* criticism. For example, some specific institution, such as duelling or the closed shop, may be criticised without criticising the whole structure of society, and such non-radical criticism is essential if there is to be any deliberate social improvement at all. This is the point of view put forward in Sir Karl Popper's *The Open Society and its Enemies*, which is conservative in so far as it emphasises the confusions and dangers in attempting to re-create society as a whole, and is at any rate less conservative in so far as the importance of criticism is emphasised. His argument is closely linked with his epistemological views, and it is interesting to consider whether investigation into the structure of knowledge and its improvement is able to throw light on the structure of society and its improvement. Descartes was an intellectual radical—for he wanted to overthrow past knowledge and start again from a basic certainty—but he was politically conservative. It has been held, however, that his intellectual radicalism helped to produce the political radicalism of the eighteenth century.

To the objection that if radicalism is really impossible it need not be warned against as conservatives say it should be, the answer is that people who think society can be radically transformed as a result of deliberate politics can do a lot of harm in the course of attempting to do the impossible. Of course they can, but may they not do a lot of good as well? J. S. Mill believed that it would be bad for everyone if either conservatives (he called them 'the party of Order') or radicals (he called them 'the party of Progress') got the upper hand to the exclusion of the others. If the first prevailed, improvements would cease to be made and a general deterioration would set in. If the second prevailed, the achievements of civilisation might be squandered away.

Considerations of this sort should lead us to ask to what extent predictions about society as a whole can be successfully made. Clearly, the radical must believe that his plans for wholesale reorganisation have a good chance of success. He must therefore, be assuming that quite large-scale predictions can be relied upon. The conservative, on the other hand, will argue that, although reliable predictions can be made within specific social fields on the assumption that other things remain as they are, it is quite different and much more dubious to rely on predictions about the whole course of social life, especially when this is to be effected by the measures proposed by the radicals. It follows that the problem of what sorts of social prediction may be reliable and what sorts of social prediction are unreliable or impossible is an important one for the issue we have been discussing, and indeed, for political philosophy as a whole. It is a problem in which logic, epistemology, the philosophy of history, and sociology are all implicated, and is hence much too complex to be taken any further in this preliminary account of it.

We have now made some comments on a long-standing controversy of wide scope and continuing interest. We have seen that in stating and clarifying the opposed points of view, and in pursuing the arguments and counter-arguments that are presented, we are forced to go into questions about temperaments, attitudes and points of view, about preserving or losing one's identity, about what sort of reasoning is proper in the context of social institutions and social change, and about the possibilities of prediction in the social sphere.

Starting, then, with one rather vague question, we have had to raise many other rather more precise ones. It is now time to take up what, to begin with, appears to be a more limited topic and to start by making use of what on p. 13 was called the method of conceptual analysis. Let us, then, try to understand, as an illustration of another problem of political philosophy, what is meant by 'equality'.

Equality

Equality is a member of the French Revolutionary Trinity,

along with Liberty and Fraternity. It is known, from what was said in the debates in the National Assembly and from what was written down in the various constitutions devised in the years from 1789 onwards, what the revolutionaries had in mind. Their meaning emerges from consideration of what they were *against*. They were against certain privileges. The church and the nobles, for example, did not have to pay the taxes that other people had to, and the population at large had no say in who should govern and what laws should be made. When, therefore, the revolutionaries of 1789 demanded equality, they meant that all people should be liable to pay taxes and that all people were entitled to play a part in electing their representatives and hence in making the laws. It was held to be wrong for the nobles to have tax and other privileges because of their birth, and for the church to receive special treatment by comparison with other associations. In brief, when equality was demanded, it was being said that *no one* ought to be excluded from carrying certain burdens (taxes) and that *everyone* ought to be a citizen and elector.

This is equality as understood in the *liberal* outlook. We may notice three important features of it:

(*a*) There are to be no exclusions, everyone is in. This has been regarded as a political expression of the Christian idea that God is equally concerned with everyone, that all men are equal in his sight. It has also been expressed as the assertion that everyone counts, or as the claim, as Kant put it, that all men have dignity. When it is said that all men are equal, it is not being said that they are *in fact* all alike in some way, but rather that they ought not to be ignored or despised or regarded merely as means to the purposes of others.

(*b*) Another feature of the view we are considering is that differences of treatment need to be justified. For example, if some people are not to pay taxes and if some people are not to have votes, there must be some good reason for this. It is a good reason for not paying taxes that the individual in question cannot afford to, and it is a good reason for not having the vote that the individual in question is insane. It is not a good reason for not paying taxes that you are a landowning peer, not a good reason for not having the vote that you have red hair. Obviously there is a lot that needs to be said about what constitute good reasons for exclusion or for difference of treatment, but the basic idea is that it is *differences* that need justification and that similarity of treatment does not need justification. We might put it briefly by saying that there is a presumption in favour of equality. (A conservative might say that there is a presump-tion in favour of the *status quo* rather than in favour of equality.)

(*c*) Although in the liberal view of equality all men have dignity and it is differences that need to be justified, liberals do not believe that all individuals should start their lives level with one another. At the time of the French Revolution liberals urged that officers' posts in the army should not be reserved for aristocrats as they had been hitherto. They believed that the poorest private soldier should not be debarred from promotion to the highest military office for which he was capable. Hence *equality of opportunity* was advocated in the sense that there were to be no legal hind-rances to success; everyone should be entitled to take any opportunities that are offered. But liberals do not suggest that all men should be *given* similar opportunities, or the same opportunities.

It was with the coming of socialist ideas that equality of property and equality of income came to be advocated. The socialist objects to a system in which incomes and chances in life are affected by the possession of inherited property or the lack of it. His objection is that this is *unjust*. It would be just for people to start equal and for their remuneration to be related to their needs and to their contributions to society. Here again, the presumption is in favour of equal property and equal remuneration, and the only justifiable differences must be because of different needs and different contributions. Differences in property and income that have come about as a result of accident, ancient institutions and the efforts of ancestors long since dead, ought to be dim-inished or eliminated, the socialist argues, in favour of a more just distribution, and this means a more equal distribution.

The concept of equality, it will be seen, is now leading us into the concept of justice. There is a close connexion between the two. A just judge treats similar cases in a similar way and does not show favour to some accused person and disfavour to others. He is impartial and keeps the scales of justice equal. The laws are administered justly when they are applied without fear or favour. If there were a law requiring all red-headed men to pay 50 per cent more taxes than all other people, then it would be justly administered if all the red-headed men and only the red-headed men were made to pay the extra tax. All the red-headed men would be treated equally in being made to pay, and all the others would be treated equally in being let off the extra. But the justice demanded by socialists, of course, goes much further than this. The laws themselves, they say, should be just and hence should favour or require a just distribution of income and property. This would require there to be considerable alterations in the distribution that chance and past efforts have brought about. There should not only be equality of opportunity in the sense of there being no hindrances to *take* opportunities but also in the sense that the opportunities presented to individuals be made equal. That is people should be *given* equal opportunities. If people inherit different amounts of property, and some people inherit none at all, and if the children of the better-off are sent to better schools than the others are, then opportunities have not been made equal and some people therefore have a better start than others.

Critics of this socialist conception of equality of opportunity argue that as it is not something that comes about naturally it would have to be organised and enforced. Parents would have to be prevented from leaving property to their children and prohibited from sending them to the schools they preferred to pay for. Furthermore, if, as seems to be the case, some people are cleverer and more energetic than others, there is a natural tendency towards inequality which those who want more equality would have to work against. Thus, to the extent that equality has to be enforced, freedom to bequeath property and to set up schools would have to be limited. Freedom in the socialist sense, therefore, is in conflict with these freedoms and, some would say, with more freedoms besides.

We have seen, then, that there is a fundamental dignity pertaining to all men in respect of which all men are said to be equal. It is differences of treatment, it is said, that need justifying and in liberal societies it is believed that there should be equality of opportunity. Justice involves equal treatment under the law and is in other ways allied to equality. (Aristotle, in the *Nicomachean Ethics,* Book V, uses the same word for equality and for justice). Socialists interpret equality of opportunity to mean that all people should be *provided with* it, whereas liberals have interpreted it to mean that all people should be free to *take* and to *make* opportunities. Hence the socialist conception of equality may come into conflict with some aspects of freedom.

Political Philosophy and the History of Ideas

It will be noticed that in both of the examples of discussions in political philosophy which we have given, reference was made to historical circumstances. Conservatism, we have pointed out, became conscious of itself when confronted by the radicalism of the French Revolution, and the liberal senses of equality can be best understood by considering what it was that the French revolutionaries were opposed to. (Incidentally, the device of asking what the opposite is of the concept we are examining is often a useful one in philosophy.) The issues and ideas of political philosophy are thus best understood in the context of their formation and use. Concepts such as 'number', 'unity' or 'quality', are much less tied to particular historical periods and activities than are such concepts as 'state', 'socialism', 'equality' or 'revolution'. (Revolutions in the sense of the seizing of power by new men have taken place since very early times, but revolution in the sense of the consciously undertaken reconstruction of the social order is a more recent conception, even though we may see anticipations of it in Plato and in sixteenth- and seventeenth-century Platonists.) If the historical context of political terms is lost sight of, then barren and even ludicrously abstract talk can be indulged in, as in the resonant vacuities about liberty and justice uttered by pompous politicians.

Appendix: Factual Matters

R. J. Hirst

FURTHER READING

The next stage for most of those who have found this book interesting should ideally be a philosophy class, but some will not be able to manage that, and even for those who do there will be a lapse of time before entering the class. We have therefore included a list of (mainly inexpensive) books suitable for further reading.

GENERAL

(i) Classics

One plan would be to see what you can make of some of the philosophical classics mentioned in this book, though they have some difficult passages. Examples of these classics are:

PLATO, *Republic* (London: Penguin Books, or any edition) which touches on a wide range of topics.

PLATO, *Phaedo* (London: Penguin Books, *'The Last Days of Socrates'*, or any other edition). On immortality and the soul.

DESCARTES, *Meditations* (London: Dent, Everyman edition entitled *Discourse on Method*; New York: Scribner's edition of *Selections from Descartes*; or Volume 1 of the Cambridge University Press paperback edition of Descartes). His most important work.

MILL, J. S., *Utilitarianism* and *On Liberty* (both in *Utilitarianism, Liberty and Representative Government*, London: Dent Everyman edition). On moral and political philosophy.

(*ii*) *History*

COPLESTON, F. C., *History of Philosophy* (London: Burns & Oates, 1952–66). In several volumes (reprinted in Doubleday Image paperback). Accurate, but not exciting.

RUSSELL, BERTRAND, *History of Western Philosophy* (London: Unwin paperback, 1963). Lively, but unfortunately misleading at times.

(*iii*) *Modern Introductions to Philosophy*

EMMET, E. R., *Learning to Philosophise* (London: Longmans, Green, 1964). Modernist with much attention to problems of meaning and misleading language.

HOSPERS, J., *Introduction to Philosophical Analysis* (London: Routledge and Kegan Paul, 1956). Very solid and informative on wide range of philosophical questions.

EDWARDS, P., and PAP, A., *A Modern Introduction to Philosophy* (New York: Collier-Macmillan, 1965). A series of readings from important discussions of some of the main philosophical problems, together with introduction and bibliography for each problem. These last two books each cover as much ground as a year's course.

MORE SPECIFIC

Logic

SALMON, W., *Logic* (Englewood Cliffs, N.J.: Prentice-Hall, 1963). A general discussion; there are many others.

QUINE, W. V. O., *Elementary Logic* (New York: Harper Torchbook, 1965). On concepts of symbolic logic.

Epistemology

RUSSELL, BERTRAND, *The Problems of Philosophy* (London: Oxford University Press, 1912, now in Opus paperback edition). Virtually a classic, some of it is dated now but it is still a clear and stimulating work by a brilliant philosopher.

AYER, A. J., *The Problem of Knowledge* (London: Penguin Books, 1956). A well-known contemporary discussion.

Metaphysics

WHITELEY, C. H. *Introduction to Metaphysics* (London: Methuen paperback, 1950). Discusses epistemology also.

TAYLOR, R., *Metaphysics* (Englewood Cliffs, N.J.: Prentice-Hall paperback, 1963). Good, but not easy.

EWING, A. C., *Fundamental Questions* (London: Routledge and Kegan Paul, 1951). Covers epistemology also.

Moral Philosophy

FRANKENA, W., *Ethics* (Englewood Cliffs, N.J.: Prentice-Hall paperback, 1963).

WARNOCK, MARY., *Ethics since 1900* (London: Oxford University paperback, *Opus I*, 1960). Neither is elementary.

Political and Social Philosophy

MABBOTT, J. D., *The State and the Citizen* (London: Hutchinson University Library paperback, 1948). A good brief introduction.

SABINE, G. H., *A History of Political Theory* (London: Harrap, 3rd edn., 1963). A more detailed history.

REQUIREMENTS FOR THE STUDY OF PHILOSOPHY

General Requirements

A wide background of general knowledge is desirable, but more important than previous study are the qualities of mind. To study philosophy successfully one needs to have:

(i) Intellectual curiosity, especially a strong interest in the kind of fundamental question discussed in philosophy; (ii) Independence of mind, i.e., an unwillingness to take things on trust, and a determination to seek the justification of views and theories and to ferret things out for oneself; (iii) Intellectual toughness and perseverance, because philosophy often seems confusing at first; there is not the mass of agreed fact that there is in so many subjects; (iv) Analytical powers—a sensitivity to implications, a feeling for meanings and shades of meaning, an ability to handle abstract ideas.

This may sound too much to expect in an entrant, but as these are powers developed by philosophical study it is their potentiality which is important.

All the same, some school subjects are more use than others, either because excellence in them is a pointer to success in philosophy or because they provide material for philosophical analysis. First among these is English, in particular Uses of English or English Language. If one is good at this, one can be expected to be good at handling ideas, to be sensitive to meanings, to be precise, and to be able to express oneself clearly. One should note that Interpretation of English papers and the like in Certificate of Education examinations may raise logical or philosophical questions, or at least provide practice in the kind of preliminary analysis found in philosophy. Aesthetic sensitivity of the 'literary' type is less valuable, but is still useful in so far as it is linked to or presupposes the linguistic sensitivity. Further, many novels, especially those classed as literature, are useful material for the moral philosopher, providing striking examples of moral conflicts and problems, with insight into human nature, motives and beliefs.

Secondly, mathematics and the mathematical sciences such as physics provide useful background and give training in precision, independence of mind and the search for valid reasons and proofs. One of the concerns of the theory of knowledge is how far mathematics provides a standard to which other knowledge should approximate, and there has been a good deal of metaphysical discussion turning on the interpretation of geometry and physics. Also, modern formal logic, though a specialised subject and only in an elementary form included in any undergraduate course, is very akin to mathematics and looks like off-beat algebra. Some school mathematical syllabuses of the first secondary year provide practice in elementary formal logic, though for analysis of actual arguments ability to appreciate subtleties of meaning and interpretation is more important.

Thirdly, Latin and Greek are also helpful, and not only in the obvious way of enabling one to read, say, Plato and Aristotle in the original; there is a further point that the idioms, technical terms and habits of thought of the Greeks and Romans were so different from those found in modern English that to translate into or from their languages requires and fosters attention to actual meanings; statements have to be recast in a way which forces one to think out carefully and precisely what was intended, and this is valuable training for philosophy.

Fourthly, history also provides evidence of human motives and behaviour which is a useful background study to moral philosophy and especially to political philosophy. Knowledge of the Renaissance background and of the rise of science is useful for epistemology and the history of philosophy.

Formal Requirements

It is only rarely that any special G.C.E. or S.C.E. requirements are laid down for entry to philosophy courses. Normally entrance qualifications for entry to the University (England) or Arts Faculty (Scotland) are enough, though there may be an interview, at least where direct entry to an honours course is required. Full information on this can be obtained from the *Compendium of University Requirements* published by the Association of Commonwealth Universities, 36 Gordon Square, London, W.C.1. Invaluable is *How to Apply for Admission to a University*, published by U.C.C.A. (Universities' Central Council on Admissions), 29 Tavistock Square, London, W.C.1. Both should be available at your school.

MODES OF INSTRUCTION AND STUDY

Lecture Courses

This is systematic instruction by lecturers to a possibly quite large class of students. It is the only way of getting across fundamental and up-to-date information to a large group and is often supplemented by duplicated 'handouts'. In general there is little opportunity for questions or discussions by the audience (except by approaching the lecturer personally).

Seminars

These are smaller groups for teaching and discussion (10 to 15 students perhaps but numbers vary). The topic for discussion is usually introduced by a short paper from a member of the class. Seminars may be geared to lectures and discuss some topic on which the lecture has just been given. Terminology varies; seminars are often called tutorials, and both may be referred to as discussion periods.

Tutorials

These are conducted by a tutor with from one to say four students. Usually a student reads an essay or shorter paper which is then discussed in detail with the tutor and any other students. A tutor also acts as general guide and adviser on the course. Some universities also have Advisers of Studies, 'Regents' or Moral Tutors, who are not limited to students of any one subject and who give advice on courses and general problems.

Private Study

Students must be prepared to do a large amount of private reading and study of recommended books and articles in periodicals. Some of this will be directed to essays and papers for tutorials, but the good student will read widely and show initiative in seeking out reading beyond the actual prescription. The change from the close control of most school work to the largely unsupervised study at a university is very difficult for some students to make. It requires a good deal of self-discipline to get into the habit of working without the stimulus of a set exercise which has to be handed in within the next day or two, but the acquisition of this self-discipline is an important part of a student's preparation for life, as well as necessary for passing examinations.

UNIVERSITY COURSES IN PHILOSOPHY

With the exception of some former technical colleges and as yet, the University of Essex, all British universities offer honours courses in philosophy. There are however significant differences. At a few universities the honours course is in philosophy alone (though with some subsidiary subjects), and at some others philosophy can only be studied jointly with some other subject at an honours level: usually, however, either possibility is open to the student. The range of subjects with which philosophy may be combined in an honours group varies a good deal. Most institutions offer philosophy with at least English, politics or psychology. There is some variety in the availability of particular subjects within the philosophy curriculum, for example Greek philosophy, aesthetics, philosophy of science, post-Kantian philosophy. The time at which one must finally decide whether to read philosophy is most important. At London and most English provincial universities this must be done on entry to university; in Scotland the decision has usually to be made at the end of the second year of a four-year course, and in Wales and at a few English universities it is made at the end of the first year of a three-year course.

There would be little point in giving all the details here since syllabus changes would soon make the lists out of date. Detailed information can be obtained, however, from two publications which are revised regularly:

1. *C.R.A.C.* (*Philosophy Degree Course Guide*)—available from

the Careers Research and Advisory Centre, Bateman Street, Cambridge. The centre also provides a 'question service' supplying information on courses, etc. to private enquirers. Many schools subscribe to the Centre's advisory service.

2. *Which University?*, published by the Cornmarket Press, (paperback, 1967). This gives summaries of university courses at the various universities in other subjects as well as in philosophy; it also provides advice on applications and brief descriptions of the various universities.

When a provisional choice has been made on the basis of the information summarised in these publications it is important, as they point out, to check with the latest edition of the university Calendar or any relevant syllabus issued by the university you favour.

CONSIDERATIONS TO BE BORNE IN MIND IN CHOOSING A UNIVERSITY

It is difficult to give any objective and non-controversial general advice on this question, but the following should be noted.

If you wish to study philosophy along with another subject make sure that the option is available; the wider the range of groups available the better since tastes and interests change after a year or so at the university. Of less importance is the range of subsidiary subjects available.

If you have specialised interests in a branch of philosophy—Greek philosophy, formal logic, etc.—make sure that opportunities for the special study are available. On the whole, though, it is better to get a good general grounding in one's first degree course and specialise later.

If you haven't finally made up your mind whether to study philosophy it is clearly better to try for some university where the final decision has not to be taken until after one or two years, during which time you will have been able to sample philosophy and other subjects.

In the publications mentioned above there is the suggestion that prospective students should take into account the influence on the character of philosophy courses exerted by individual professors and other teachers and by the balance of tutorials, seminars and lectures. To this end, one of them mentions the present posts of certain well-known philosophers. This however can be very misleading. University staffs are continually changing (of the 8 well-known philosophers mentioned outside Oxford, 4 were 18 months later no longer teaching at the universities attributed to them); prominent personalities in philosophy may be little concerned in undergraduate teaching especially tutorials, either as a matter of university regulation, or because of absence on lecture tours or visiting professorships, or from the pressure of their other interests; their reputation may well depend on their publications and not on their teaching ability. In general it is almost impossible for the outsider to assess the 'character' of a university course (though detailed study of its syllabus is some help), but it is doubtful whether this matters much at an undergraduate level. Certainly all philosophers are convinced that discussion with students is essential to the teaching of the subject, and most departments try to strike the balance they think best between lectures, seminars and tutorials. Sometimes the staff/student ratio prevents an ideal balance, but that is a very variable factor. Most departments nowadays are democratic in that syllabuses are discussed with and influenced by all the staff and not just dictated by the professor. (There is advice on such points in K. Boehm, *University Choice,* which also gives a very brief account of each of the various university subjects.)

One factor that does vary greatly from university to university is the size of the philosophy staffs. Large staffs mean that the student will find a wide range of interests and stimulating clashes of views among the staff, as well as a large number of other students to discuss things with, but a small staff with a few students can give more individual attention.

The staff at British universities are listed by university and departments in the *Handbook of Universities of the British Commonwealth* which should be available in your local reference library. In the entry for some universities philosophy is covered by two or more departments, so that staff may be under Logic (and Metaphysics), Moral Philosophy, Political Philosophy, or just Philosophy. Even though revised annually, the handbook cannot keep up with staff changes. Student numbers, however, are difficult to discover. Most universities publish honours degree results in their Calendars (so you can see how many obtained the degree), but some universities have large first-year classes in philosophy for those reading other subjects, and these may make large demands on staff time. If you have an interview you may be able to learn about numbers and facilities generally.

Another important factor, though one difficult to assess beforehand, is the strength of the university and departmental libraries both in range of books held and, where there is an appreciable number of students, in the number of duplicates of important books available. On the whole the older universities have the advantage here, since they could buy books and numbers of periodicals (many now out of print) when they were available. Reprints of periodicals are now becoming available but are very expensive, and this has made it more difficult for new institutions to build up their libraries.

CAREERS

The intrinsic advantages of philosophical study have been indicated in the *Introduction*—the opportunity it gives to clarify one's ideas on fundamental problems, to get to know the main lines of solution that have been put forward and to understand and assess their strength and weaknesses. There is also the further advantage that all this is excellent mental training in the analysis of problems and in stating and assessing a case. In any top job a good deal of time is devoted to writing, examining and evaluating reports on a wide range of topics, and the critical study of philosophical theses is very good practice for this. But the student will naturally want to know what all this can mean in terms of an actual career, and anyhow in the early stages before these advantages become apparent it is helpful to know where it all may lead.

Of course if one turns out to be really good at and interested in philosophy there is no particular problem. With first or very good second-class honours in philosophy, whether philosophy alone or jointly with another subject, one can hope to pass on to research and a second degree in philosophy and then to a university teaching post. But the majority of students will not attain this; so what then? A lot depends on the part philosophy plays in one's degree. If philosophy is a subsidiary subject to honours in something else or to a general or ordinary degree, the career will depend on what else was studied. To a large extent this will be true of joint honours degrees, i.e. philosophy studied equally with some other subject such as English, mathematics or economics. That indeed is a good argument for taking a joint degree; if one's philosophy is not exceptionally good one can then rely on the other subject for bread and butter. Thus philosophy/English students may go on to teach English in schools. Furthermore there is a range of teaching posts in general studies in technical colleges or technical universities, and while one may obtain one of these with a pure philosophy degree, honours study of English or one of the social sciences is a distinct advantage. And if one is thinking of a career in industry, the factual knowledge required in the study of economics is a valuable adjunct to the mental training given in philosophy. Another good reason for a joint degree is that the study of some other subject is beneficial to the philosopher. It provides him with useful raw material in the form of philosophical problems raised in a context he understands, and with evidence about human nature or science which throw light on philosophical questions. At the same time his philosophical training will improve the analytical power he brings to the other subjects.

For those who have honours in philosophy alone the situation is a little more difficult. Some, of course, study philosophy as a preparation to second degree in law or theology. Certainly philosophy is good training for either of these, but two degrees are not always financially possible. Possible career openings after a pure philosophy honours degree, besides university or technical college teaching or perhaps a post in industry, are listed below.

The Civil Service

At the top is the Administrative Grade for which there are two methods of entry: Method I, consisting in a qualifying examination plus special subject papers, and Method II, a qualifying examination plus selection board. For the qualifying examination philosophy is very useful, one-third of the crucial General Paper consisting of arguments for logical analysis. Of the 7 special subject papers, up to 6 may be philosophical, while one must, and more may be, taken from some other subject (no doubt one's subsidiary or joint honours subject). With first class honours or a post-graduate degree in philosophy you can by-pass the qualifying examination for Method II. With a 'first' you may get exemption from the special papers under Method I. At a lower level there are posts as Income Tax Inspectors or Ministry of Labour Cadets and various positions in the Executive grade open to philosophical graduates who pass a further examination and/or interview. For further details see the booklet, *Civil Service Posts for Graduates*, published annually by the Civil Service Commission and obtainable from H.M. Stationery Office.

University administration

There are openings here for graduates in any subject.

Librarianship

In university libraries graduates are sought and the philosophically trained mind is useful; sometimes in university libraries, and almost invariably in others, a specialised qualification in librarianship is required; this can be obtained after graduation and grants are normally available.

Computer programming and data processing

This kind of work is often very suitable for those with logical, mathematical or philosophical training, though special aptitude tests may be required. As this is such a new and rapidly expanding field most training is done 'on the job', but some specialised training centres or 'schools of computing' now offer short courses and aptitude tests. And there has now even been published *Teach Yourself Computer Programming.*

Social work

There are a number of openings here for those attracted to it; while sympathetic interest in fellow human beings is essential, so also is a balanced outlook which will mitigate the danger of becoming emotionally involved in one's clients' problems. Hence philosophical training plus a subsidiary or joint honours subject in the social sciences is suitable, but a year at least of specialised training is required after graduation.

Other posts

For those with the appropriate literary or artistic talents, as well as philosophical training, posts are available in the B.B.C., British Council, journalism, advertising, etc. But there is severe competition for these.

There are merely suggestions to be borne in mind when considering whether to take philosophy and, if so, then whether to take joint honours or which subsidiary subjects to study. More specific advice governed by knowledge of your particular abilities must be obtained from your university Appointments Officer.

Index